A KLONDIKE CHRISTMAS

EDITED BY

Anne Tempelman-Kluit

A KLONDIKE CHRISTMAS

CELEBRATING THE SEASON IN A NORTHERN FRONTIER

WHITECAP BOOKS

VANCOUVER / TORONTO

The information contained in this book is true and complete to the best of our
knowledge. All recommendations are made without guarantee on the part of the
author or Whitecap Books Ltd. The author and publisher disclaim any liability in
connection with the use of this information. For additional information please
contact Whitecap Books Ltd., 351 Lynn Avenue, North Vancouver, BC, V7J 2C4.

Every effort has been taken to trace the ownership of copyright material used in the
text. The author and publisher welcome any information enabling them to rectify
any reference or credit in subsequent editions.

Copy-edited by Elizabeth McLean
Cover design by Bradbury Design
Cover illustration by Ted Harrison
Interior design by Warren Clark
Interior illustrations by Darlene Fletcher

Printed In Canada

Canadian Cataloguing in Publication Data
A klondike christmas

    Includes bibliographical references.
    ISBN 1-55110-770-8

    1. Christmas—Yukon Territory—Klondike River Valley—
Literary collections. 2. Klondike River Valley (Yukon)—Gold Discoveries—
Literary collections. 3. Canadian literature (English)*
I. Tempelman-Kluit, Anne, 1941–
GT4987.15.K56 1998   C810.8'0334   C98-910661-6

The publisher acknowledges the support of the Canada Council for the Arts for our
publishing program and the Cultural Services Branch of the Government of British
Columbia in making this publication possible. We acknowledge the financial support
of the Government of Canada through the Book Industry Development Program for
our publishing activities.

For more information on other titles from
Whitecap Books, visit our web site at www.whitecap.ca

For my parents, who travelled far,
but never North,
and for Frances, Vija and Akron
for one particularly memorable trip
to Dawson.

Acknowledgments

Few books are the work of one person; this one is no exception. Some of the people who helped and whom I thank are Sally Bremner for enthusiasm, Paul Grescoe for sage advice, Karin Waterreus and Bente Sorensen for help with critical details. I also thank Nick Read, Veronica Woodruff, Isobel Nanton, Andrew Costen and Judi Lees for humor and support. Special thanks go to the staff of Special Collections at the Vancouver Public Library, the B.C. Archives and Records Service, the Yukon Archives, Yukon College Library and the Whitehorse Public Library for patience and helpfulness. Lewis Green helped solve a puzzle, Annemarie helped organize me and Nadaleen dug for stories with inspiration. As always, thanks to my husband Dirk, who knows his way around computers almost as well as he knows his way around the Yukon.

Contents

Introduction

O ccasionally, life brings you a gift of the unexpected. For me, the Yukon was that gift. I knew nothing about what seemed a lonely, unpeopled land—physically and psychologically such a long way from anywhere. A particularly long way from London, England, my home before coming to Canada.

When, in 1964, I first went to Dawson City to visit my geologist husband I was intrigued by the hot, dusty little community cradled between the Klondike and the Yukon rivers. The river smells mingled with the aroma of warm wood from the weathered, sagging Gold Rush–era buildings lining Second Avenue. Fireweed grew through gaps in the boardwalk and through the gaping windows of deserted houses and dark log cabins. But there were also trim homes, their gardens bright with flowers and vegetables.

Farther back from the river were more cramped cabins, many with their roofs fallen in, but moose horns still bravely guarded empty doorways. Outside one cabin hung a heavy leather horse harness; another held a tiny, painted carving of a house in the mountains; beside another was a small, disintegrating leather boot. Newspapers were stuffed into gaps between the logs and used as wallpaper and for insulation. One just-legible newspaper mentioned casualties of a First World War skirmish and wished readers "Christmas joys."

Years later, while living in Whitehorse and working as a reporter for the *Whitehorse Star*, I was

1899 map of Klondike area.

researching in the Yukon Archives and came across a listing: "Christmas—Klondike." That desolate little cabin in Dawson and its newspaper-covered wall flashed through my mind, along with the little boot. How had that child celebrated Christmas in the Klondike? Were there gifts, special treats and socializing, or was life so hard that it was a day like any other? The idea for this book was born.

Our family Yukon Christmases were all special—one Yukon friend comments "cold climate, warm friends"— made up of sledding parties, blazing bonfires and hot chocolate, cross-country ski picnics, skating parties and mulled wine. We remember one special Christmas Eve when we walked home from a neighborhood party. It was about twenty degrees below and, other than the squeak of the snow beneath our boots, quite silent. Bright stars glittered coldly above us; snow crystals sparkled in the welcoming glow of lamplit windows; from somewhere in the nearby forest came the eerie yipping of coyotes. Our goose bumps were not from the cold. On other occasions the Northern Lights held us spellbound as streamers of green and gold and blue wove their magic across the sky. In the coldest, darkest time of the year Christmas was a celebration of warmth and light, a time to cherish family and friends and to dream new dreams.

Dreams of gold lured thousands of men—and a handful of women—from across the world to the promised riches of the Klondike in the summer of 1898. If any gave Christmas a thought, it was probably with expectations of returning home laden with gold dust and gleaming nuggets. Most discovered nothing, except perhaps a sense of fulfillment at having completed an incredible journey. As their hopes of riches faded, they faced a long, lonely winter far from home.

But there was a Christmas that year. While working on articles and other projects I came across stories which periodically reminded me of my Christmas book idea; some are in this book. Finally I plunged into Gold Rush Christmases, and into the lives of hundreds of men and women who had a golden dream, and the faith and courage to follow it North. The stories included here span a period from 1882 to 1926, but most are drawn from the Gold Rush days of 1897 to 1902. I have collected the recipes in this book over the years; they seem appropriate given the emphasis on Christmas feasts in many of the stories. The recipes reflect Gold Rush times in the scarcity of ingredients; if you try one you may want to modify it for today.

Researching Christmas was fascinating. Books, letters, diaries, files of cards, pamphlets, anything about life in, or on the way to, the gold fields might mention Christmas—or might not. It was mostly the miners, their wives and the later arrivals in the Klondike who cared enough and had time to record their Christmas experiences. Some stories led to others, some leads were dead ends, but following the paper trails introduced me to wonderful people with Gold Rush connections. One delightful lady, Lucille Hooker, aged 105, was seven when she and her mother climbed the Chilkoot Trail on the way to meet her father in Dawson. When I spoke with her in Vancouver recently she recalled her first Christmas in the Klondike. "The children went to a party at the Methodist Hall. They brought in a dog team and snow. We saw dog teams and snow every day, but we'd never seen them indoors! That was special."

That is why these stories are special. Not only for their intrinsic value, or for how Christmas was celebrated, but for where it was celebrated and that it was celebrated at all. Thousands of miles from home and family, despite isolation, despite lack of provisions, despite the brutal cold, these adventurers held close to the Yuletide traditions of their homelands. These are stories of hope and gentle humor, and of the warmth of friendship and sharing—the spirit of Christmas.

Greeting

Xmas. Dawson City: Yukon Ter. 1898

 o my friends of the great Klondike, Yukon and Copper River Co., as well as to all my other friends, in grateful remembrance of their many acts of kindness, and also for that confidence which has sustained me amid trying scenes of toil and danger, on the snow-clad trail to the Yukon Gold District.

Accept this little Christmas token,
Rustic shadow of your friend,
Purest thoughts are oft unspoken,
Sunshine oft with shadows blend.
So today among the mountains,
Thoughts that cannot be expressed,
Bubble up from natures fountains,
In a corner of my breast.

And I feel the sunshine twinkling
Through the icy atmosphere,
While the Christmas bells are tinkling,
Tolling—Christ again is here.
Faith and hope were never stronger,
Since I started up life's hill,
I can wait, and hope, yet longer,
Aye, and trust the Master still.

Yours in Clouds and Sunshine,
J.W. Crawford

Captain Jack Crawford was a popular "poet-scout," dandy and trader in Dawson during the Gold Rush. His poems about everyday events and people, composed at the drop of a hat, were in great demand.

Dinner on Miller Creek

by Emilie Tremblay, as told to Father Marcel Bobillier OMI

My husband, Jack Tremblay, had come to Cohous, New York, from Alaska for a visit in 1894 [….] We were married there, and three days later we were on our way to the North. I had never traveled, except to New York from Quebec, where I was born, and I couldn't talk English.

It was all new and strange. He had a claim and a cabin near Fortymile on the Yukon. To get there we had to go to Dyea, and then over the Chilkoot Pass, and then to the Yukon. It took us three months from the time we left Seattle on the old steamship *Topeka* in the spring.

Turn-of-the-century cabin.

The cabin was little. It had been built of logs, with beer bottles placed in the walls for windows and half of the floor was just packed dirt. It had a fireplace for cooking, and bunks, and that was about all. We stayed there through the winter of 1894 and 1895.

As I was the only woman at Miller Creek, during that winter of 1894–95, I decided, with my husband, to invite all the miners and prospectors living in the neighbourhood for Christmas. They were about a dozen.

All our winter's supplies had been brought in by Jack and his employees on their backs. Those supplies therefore were limited. As for the kitchen utensils, we had only the minimum, that is, two plates, two spoons, two forks and two knives.

We had plenty of meat. Caribou was plentiful and the jackrabbits abounded in the vicinity. The meat question was settled, although we had not enough dishes to serve it.

As for vegetables, I would prepare a big pot of beans and for dessert, I would have a prune pudding.

Using some birch bark for paper, I sent an invitation to all miners to attend our supper on Christmas Day at 6:00 p.m. At the bottom of the invitation I added, "Bring your own spoon, fork and knife."

The biggest problem for me was to cook enough meat for all those men. My stove measured only 22 by 22 inches and in the narrow oven, I could place a pan only six inches wide.

It was not a question of money—we had plenty of it—but of transport. How could you bring a big stove over the mountains in a place like Miller Creek? I prepared a caribou roast, cooked the rabbits shot by my husband for the occasion and baked some scones on the hot ashes of the fireplace.

And here is the menu of that famous dinner, shared by twelve men:

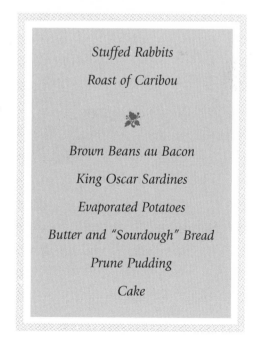

Stuffed Rabbits

Roast of Caribou

Brown Beans au Bacon

King Oscar Sardines

Evaporated Potatoes

Butter and "Sourdough" Bread

Prune Pudding

Cake

These evaporated potatoes replaced in those days the real tubercles too heavy to carry and so easy to freeze.

The pudding was also made of dried prunes with a blueberry sauce. Egg powder, instead of fresh eggs, went into the baking of the cake.

No matter how hard it is to believe that such a meal could be produced in such a place and in those days, it is a fact that it was done.

In my wardrobe, I took one of those long skirts, whose use was then fashionable, a skirt I had never worn. I cut it up and used it as a table cloth.

One prospector was missing when all our guests had arrived. Some said he had been gone for two or three days. We sat down to dinner. At the end of the meal, who should arrive but the missing guest who put a bottle of rum on the table? He had walked thirty miles in the snow to go and buy that bottle and had walked thirty miles back to bring it to us and enhance our little celebration.

After dinner, we played cards and I gave the miners permission to smoke. They all hastened to fill up their pipes, for there were no cigarettes in those days. And they smoked so much that the whole cabin was shrouded in an opaque cloud of blue smoke.

We were happy to have spent such a nice Christmas dinner and evening together. All the miners went home late, taking with them their own cabin utensils.

From "Madame Emilie Tremblay: A Pioneer Woman of the Yukon," a manuscript of unpublished memoirs as told to Father Bobillier.
   Emilie Fortin from Quebec met and married a Miller Creek miner, Pierre-Nolasque (Jack) Tremblay. She arrived in the Yukon in 1894, one of twenty white women amongst a thousand men. In 1913 she opened a fashionable dress store in Dawson; it is a historical landmark.

Christmas Thoughts

by George Carmack

Christmas Eve, 1888

I'm camped on a mountain side to-night
one hundred miles from the sea,
And the smell of the caribou steak on
the coals, is a grateful odor to me.
For the deer were fleet-footed and strong
today and I've roamed the mountain's breast,
Till the bear skin robe on my cosy bed
seems beckoning me to rest.
But a tall old Spruce by the camp-fire's
glow bows his glittering top to me,
And seems to whisper, "Tis Christmas Eve
and I am your Christmas Tree."
Then a flood of memories o'er me sweeps
and my spirit afar doth roam
To where there's another glittering tree,
in a California home.
There all is light and life and love and
the children laugh with glee,
And I cannot but wonder with wistful
pain are they thinking to-night of me?
But a whisper comes from the tall old
Spruce and my soul from pain is free,
For I know when they kneel together tonight
they'll all be praying for me.

"From an old memorandum book is taken a few lines written by the wanderer on Christmas, 1888 when in his mountain habitat, far from civilization and many miles from the track of any living man." The *Klondike News:* April 1898.

George Carmack's discovery of gold sparked the Klondike Gold Rush. He was born in California in 1860 and prospected in Alaska and the Yukon for eleven years before striking it rich on Rabbit Creek on August 17, 1896. He renamed the creek Bonanza.

Mrs. Bompas's Tree

by Mrs. William Bompas

My next grand effort was a Christmas-tree for the children of the colony. Such a thing had not only not been seen, but never heard of before, and as whispers of it went abroad the excitement and curiosity it awakened were past description. I set my heart on giving a present to every child, both white and Indian.

The Whites are chiefly the children of the officers at the Fort, and to them I could not, of course, offer clothes, so I had to manufacture toys and other small gifts out of no materials. Years ago, in my childhood, when my busy fingers accomplished things of this kind, my dear mother used to tell me I should one day be head of a toy-shop. How little did she dream in what way her words would be fulfilled! I actually made a lamb "Mackenzie River breed" all horned and woolly, with sparkling black eyes. Also dolls, painted and dressed. One infant in a moss bag like the babies here. Some dancing

Bishop and Mrs. William Bompas with a native girl.

men moved by strings, one sailor, which was my best. Also I produced, though not made by me, only under my direction, a whip with carved handle, and a drum, also balls, work cases, etc. Then I had some aprons and leggings for the servant girls and some that were left of the beautiful gifts from England for the Indians. In all I had about forty presents on the tree.

The chief difficulty was, first, candles to light it up (as all our grease had failed). I petitioned Mr. Hardisty the head officer of the Fort for "just a little grease" and he kindly sent me his very last bladderful containing some six or eight pounds. Then I set our good-natured little blacksmith (an Orkney man) to work to make us some pretty little tin moulds, by means of which I was able to manufacture some small candles, large enough to burn about half an hour.

The second difficulty was the tree itself, for which I sent men out to search. Plenty of trees there were, pretty dark firs, but so thickly laden with snow that the branches were bent down to the very ground. However, this difficulty was met, a fine young tree was found and the snow shaken off its branches, after which they resumed their natural shape. The tree was cut down as near the ground as possible, and we found an old milking tub which was deep enough to hold it and give a good, broad margin around the stem. We were nearly all day dressing the tree, which I had placed in the kitchen. Mr. Hodgson, the schoolmaster, who was most helpful to me, made a beautiful text for one end of the room, "Peace on earth and goodwill towards men." He also made me some clever little stands for the candles and some flags, etc. We dressed the rooms as well as we could with fir as our only evergreen.

At four o'clock the great bell sounded, which announced the guests were to arrive. The whole neighbourhood had been on the tiptoe of expectation; new dresses had been made, and the most elaborate toilettes invented for "Mrs. Bompas Christmas tree" which meant—no one knew what!

I received my guests, parents and children, in the drawing room, and in a few minutes marshalled the whole company into the kitchen. Do you remember the burst of rapture from the children at Bishop Tawton's in 1868 at our memorable Christmas-tree, and how it repaid us for all our toil and trouble? The delight and enthusiasm were no less manifest here, though the children in these frozen regions are usually less demonstrative than us. I made them join hands and form a circle around the tree, the little ones inside and the parents forming an outer ring. The poor Indian mothers [...] squatted down in a bunch on the floor, with faces radiant from astonishment and delight. Then I began to strip the tree and to distribute the presents, all of which, I am glad to say gave great satisfaction. Then I gave them tea and biscuits all around, and we sang some carols which I had taught the school children, and so the evening ended, and I must confess it was a very happy one.

Roast Rabbit

Skin and clean rabbit.
Put in roasting pan.
Season with salt and pepper and onion, and cover with grease or slices of bacon.
Cover and roast in slow oven for 3 hours.
Remove cover for last half hour of cooking to brown.
Baste occasionally.
Stuff if desired.

From *Five Pioneer Women of the Anglican Church in the Yukon.*
   Born and brought up in England and Europe, Charlotte Bompas lived a life of comfort before she joined her husband, the Anglican Bishop William Bompas, in the Klondike in 1892. She worked tirelessly with her husband at Forty-Mile and at Caribou Crossing (later Carcross). The couple were greatly admired by the miners. The Christmas before they left Forty-Mile, they were presented with a three-ounce gold nugget and a memorial signed by fifty-three miners "as a mark of respect and esteem from the miners of Forty-Mile irrespective of creeds or religions and as a personal present to the first white lady who has wintered amongst us."

The Christmas Caribou

by Anton Money

inter had clamped down in earnest now. The open water of the lake froze and snow lay deep over the land. The temperature hovered at around forty below, dropping down to fifty or sixty now and then. I piled up a big reserve of stove wood.

One morning I harnessed the dogs and set out to explore the upper end of Frances Lake, above the delta of the Finlayson. The dogs and I had traveled about a dozen miles, following a small frozen river beyond the head of the lake, when I saw a band of wild sheep licking at clay banks a short distance ahead. I had found a natural salt lick. The sheep had come down from a mountain to the west and their trails were all over the place. If I had had any doubt about a supply of fresh meat for the remainder of the winter, it was ended now. The salt-hungry sheep would use this place until spring, and of all the wild meat available in that country theirs was the most flavorful.

I shot two of them, dressed them, loaded the carcasses on the toboggan, and turned the dogs back toward the cabin. That was a jubilant homecoming, in the failing light of a cold winter afternoon.

By this time I had taken the floats off my gill net and stretched it under the ice of the lake a hundred feet from shore. I was catching all the whitefish I and the dogs could use, and now and then a lake trout. To lift the net I chopped a hole in the ice around the poles that anchored each end of it and pulled it out onto the ice, allowing a rope at the other end to pay out. When I had retrieved my catch, I pulled it back under the ice with that rope and anchored it again with the poles.

A few days after I had found the sheep lick I saw a band of caribou strung out across the lake three or four miles down from the cabin. They had come down the Il-es-tooa River, following the low brush on which they feed in winter. I watched them through my powerful field glasses as they crossed the lake. There must have been three hundred of them, romping and playing in the thirty-below clear air. Some of the young ones ran out from the herd, and, kicking up the snow as they ran, skidded suddenly to a stop, quickly turning their heads to see the spray of snow they had created. Some lunged with their antlers against others, in mock battle, like children playing on the school lot back home, then backed off, only to repeat it again and again. I watched them play, sometimes one throwing another down, then prancing around in the joy of victory until the conquered would leap up and give chase across the lake ice.

Seeing them play like one big family with not a care in the world made me feel suddenly very lonely. With the knowledge that Christmas was only a few days off, the sight and silence touched some key of memory and I found myself reflecting on Christmas days full of joy and laughter I had enjoyed in my childhood, surrounded by my family. Somehow, I thought, if I could join those happy caribou, if I could touch them and talk to them, it would give me a sense of companionship.

Knowing that they would stampede from a strange scent, I made plans. Early the next morning I hitched up my dogs to the toboggan, and armed with pick and shovel, mushed up the frozen lake and river to the salt lick. I broke loose a few hundred pounds of the frozen muck and loaded it onto the toboggan. The next day I mushed down the lake to the delta of the Il-es-tooa. I broke the salty clay chunks and spread them out among the caribou brush. Knowing that my scent would be where I had touched the brush, I could only hope that the caribou would tolerate the man scent in their anxiety to lick salt.

The next day, looking through my field glasses, I saw the leader come, gingerly at first, then apparently approving. He began to lick. Almost immediately the rest of the herd followed. In threes and fives and scattered throughout, they stumbled out from the shelter of the poplar trees onto the delta, and began licking the salt, nibbling occasionally at the brush. Every once in a while one of them would raise his head with a jerk, and I could almost hear him snort as he touched brush scented by man, but he would settle back and lick his beloved salty clay.

The next day I mushed up the river again and recovered more salt from the lick. It was an all-day job, twenty-four miles round trip, but the trail was hard packed from the day before and the dogs wagged their bushy tails high over their backs all day. Before turning into bed I marked off the day with an X on the calendar. Tomorrow would be Christmas Eve. The cold weather was holding so it would likely stay clear the next few days. In the morning the dogs jumped and barked as I took the harness off its pegs on the cabin wall.

We ran the few miles to the delta again, and I planted the salt as before, scattering it widely over the delta; then I went home and tied the dogs to their kennels. It was already quite dark and the stars were bright when I got back to the cabin. Tomorrow would be Christmas Day, and I would try a lonely experiment.

Before true daylight I snowshoed down the lake to the Il-es-tooa, made myself comfortable under a big poplar, and waited for the caribou.

Unless you have seen a herd of three or four hundred caribou, you have little idea of the fearlessness of the herd. They will face and kill a pack of wolves or any natural enemy. Could the desire for salt overcome the fear of man scent? This was the test. I went unarmed except for my belt knife, which is as much a part of a woodsman's clothing as his shirt. I waited, getting colder by the minute in the stillness of thirty below, for what seemed hours. Then, quite casually, there they came.

Over the brow of the upper gravel terraces I saw the leader, his magnificent spread of antlers silhouetted against the cloudless blue sky, slowly threading his way through the light growth of trees. Closely following came his herd, feeding as they came. Unhurried, nipping the tops off the brush that stuck out through the two feet of snow, and digging the snow occasionally with the shovel-like horn growth that protrudes down over their noses, they slowly came closer to me. The big bull leader must have been twenty yards from me when he jerked up his head and snorted, turning back toward the herd. I feared they would stampede, but the big bull hesitated and in a moment turned back and cautiously came closer to me. He touched the first block of frozen salt and began to lick.

I had filled my parka pockets with table salt, in case they got close enough to me. Perhaps it was wishful thinking, but there was no one to see my foolishness. I was alone with the caribou. Slowly they came, edging closer as they grazed. I stood frozen still, my hands deep in my parka pockets. My only concern was that the caribou not be afraid of me. I only wanted greatly to be friends and to understand better these carefree, happy animals.

Soon they were licking the salt blocks all around me. One, a small bull, came up close to me, and I ventured to hold out my hand full of table salt. At my arm movement he reared up and I thought for a moment that he meant to strike me down. Shaking his head, he backed off a few steps and then resumed licking salty clay, eyeing me the while. Another caribou came close,

between the first bull and me. He seemed less fearful, coming so close that I could almost reach him with an outstretched hand. I moved, tossing a little free salt. His head came up instantly, but he did not move his legs, and slowly he resumed licking. I had won. The desire for salt had overcome the fear of human scent and even the sight of me.

I stepped out from my tree in slow motion. Gingerly I approached the nearest caribou. To my surprise and joy he seemed undisturbed. Slowly I held out a handful of table salt. He leaned his beautiful antlered head down, sniffing from a foot away. Frozen, hardly breathing, I stood stock still, keeping my outstretched hand steady. The beautiful head leaned out, as I prayed that it would, and he licked the salt from my hand.

Have you ever had great faith in something, and had your innermost desire answered? It is a wonderful and most satisfying thing. To feel the confidence of that cold and wet nose snuffing into my hand of salt, an animal truly of the wilderness, unafraid, licking my hand—what a glorious, triumphant, happy feeling! I had a terrific sense of accomplishment, of being at one with all of nature.

That moment will live with me forever. Calmly I moved slowly into the herd. For a long time I *walked* with the herd as they grazed out to the lake's edge, licking the salt blocks everywhere. None seemed to fear me; I was accepted as one of them. Shuffling my snowshoes ahead quietly and avoiding any quick movement I was able to move among them—holding out my hand with its salt to one after another—and have them lick it clean. As I moved out onto the lake ice they followed.

Even as I left them, snowshoeing over my broken trail toward the cabin three miles away, one or two followed close, looking for more salt. Indeed, God was in His Heaven that Christmas Day.

That day was mine.

From *This Was the North.*
   Anton Money, a twenty-two-year-old Englishman, came to the Yukon after the Gold Rush. He successfully prospected in southeastern Yukon on Money Creek, which flows into Frances Lake.

Celebrations at Fort Reliance 1882

by Leroy N. McQuesten

hristmas we had a [snow] shovelling match and the one that got beat had to stand on his head. Mr. Carr was beaten and to the surprise of all he stood on his head and I think he was the only one in the party that could. We had a foot race and Mr. Carr won the prize. We had a good dinner and all of the Indians that were near the Station had all they wanted to eat.

New Year I gave the Indians ammunition to celebrate on and they had a splendid time. The Indians got a large moose skin and as many as could get

around it would take hold of the edge and then some young Indian would get on top of the skin and they would toss him up. The white men thought it great sport and they joined in the game.

After awhile the men began to throw the women in the moose skin and toss them up. After the women had been tossed they turned to and caught the white men and they had to take their turn to be thrown up in the air—it was great sport for those not in the moose skin as a man is perfectly helpless when he is thrown ten [feet] up.

Sometimes he will come down on his head but they never got hurt. That practice has been kept up at Forty Mile ever since. When the Indians are all there and the whites always joined in the sport and everyone living near the town had to be tossed up and they most all took their medicine in good humor.

From the *Whitehorse Star*.
Leroy N. McQuesten arrived in the Yukon well before the Gold Rush, and before there was a Dawson City. He could turn his hand to almost anything and had roamed widely through the Yukon before opening a trading post at Fort Reliance, a few miles downriver from the present site of Dawson. He was a friend to the miners and often extended them credit, trusting them to repay him with gold dust from their claims.

Klondike Santa Claus

by William Haskell

They actually got up a party at the post, and had a Christmas tree, and games, and a real old-fashioned time, indicating that the Klondike region had advanced some in civilization. It all came about through the efforts of the Rev. James Naylor, an Episcopal minister who had buried himself in the Klondike, and had devoted his life to work among the Indians [....]

Having taught them the meaning of Christmas, Mr. Naylor decided to show them that it was a time to be joyful by giving a party in which Santa Claus was to make his initial bow to a mixed audience of whites and [natives], and go through his customary performance of distributing toys and other gifts. The weather was all that Santa Claus could have desired.

But where could they get toys in that region, where every one was only too thankful to procure sufficient to eat and wood enough to cook it when procured? It happened in a strange way, but it is perhaps not so strange when one observes how many seemingly useless things gold-seekers bring into this country. One man with a trading instinct had come into the Klondike region late in the fall, and had stuffed into his pack several toys and other nicknacks where he ought to have put food. But it came out all right. Every white mother in the country around was willing to pay its weight in gold for any pitiful looking toy that bore the trademark of a city store. The man sold his toys and candy at his own prices, and was not such a freak after all. In this way Santa Claus was enabled to keep his contract with the little folks in the Klondike that year.

When the day came and the people around drove over to the mission where the party was to be given, the thermometer was at its Klondike lowest, and frost-bites threatened any nose that showed itself beyond the fur. Teams consisting of half a dozen dogs were rigged up, and women and children enveloped in furs to their eyebrows climbed in, and off they went over the hills and the frozen river with the dogs trotting along at their best pace to the door where Mr. Naylor awaited them. Inside all was merriment and laughter. The members of the little [...] colony, about a score of children, were in such

a state of gleeful expectation that they were ready to stand on their heads at the slightest provocation, and they did this at every fresh arrival. They were all gotten up in their Sunday best, but some of the white children who had come in had to waddle about in their fur boots.

Nothing like that Christmas tree was ever seen in the Klondike before. There were real dolls gaily attired, and with real eyes and noses instead of the featureless baseball heads with which the Klondike children had been forced to satisfy themselves. There were horses and wagons, dancing figures, and tiny drums, and other contrivances which bring joy to the juvenile heart, no matter in what latitude it beats. The toys were packed in bags made from mosquito netting, which was the only material available. Then Santa Claus came down and distributed them. How the little eyes of the [children] stuck out! They thought he was the genuine article. He was gotten up for Yukon weather in a great furry "parka" with the hood turned up around his face. In lieu of a genuine white beard he had powdered his own beard with flour, and no one of the children knew who he was, so effectually was he disguised. He distributed the toys to the great delight of the [children], who, after a time, could scarcely express their feelings, even by standing on their heads.

After that they went in for a series of old-fashioned games, of which blind-man's-buff proved the favorite. The mission house was built of rough untrimmed logs, like all the best houses, but some attempt had been made to decorate the interior, and with light and warmth and the merriment of happy children, it needed no very great stretch of the imagination to forget the white and frozen earth outside, and fancy ourselves at home again. The party broke up about midnight—the first genuine Christmas party, so far as I have heard, in the country of the Klondike.

From *Two Years in the Klondike and Alaskan Gold Fields*.
    William Haskell's lively and informative book about his gold mining adventures travelling to and in the Klondike is one of the most accurate and entertaining accounts of the time. The final chapter of the book contains sage advice, and a vast shopping list, for the novice stampeder.

Christmas at Moosehide

by V. H.

omen used to get together, they used to make quilts, they did a lot of beadwork. I remember my mother, when Christmas time coming, used to make all my brothers and sisters moccasins for the dance, real fancy, the *drithan* moccasins, that's what you call caribou legging moccasins. Made out of caribou leg. Used to only take her one week to make those moccasins.

by Gerald Isaac

 remember the seasonal celebrations, especially around Christmas, New Year's and Easter time. We always received visitors from Fort McPherson who came into the village by dog team. The dog teams—I'll never forget them. They were so beautifully ornamented with beadwork, pompoms and silver bells. The dog teams were just beautiful! When the Fort McPherson people came into the village of Moosehide, it was a real exciting gathering. The celebrations between Christmas and New Year's would go on for almost two weeks, day and night non-stop, the feasting, the

cooking, the dancing and the excitement at the community hall was just tremendous. I remember being there with my grandmother at these happy occasions. When I became tired, grandmother fixed a blanket bed on the bench and I crawled in for a sleep. The women would cook and the men would supply the firewood. They also played the fiddles, the drums, and other instruments and generally had a good time. They called square dancing, jigging and waltzing. Buckets of loose hard candy were thrown on stage for the children to compete for and presents were distributed as well. A good time was had by all.

From "Moosehide: An Oral History, 1994."
During the Gold Rush, the widely respected Chief Isaac guided the native village of Moosehide. Gerald Isaac is his grandson.

Bannock

2 cups flour
generous pinch of salt
2 teaspoons baking powder
2 tablespoons lard or grease
handful raisins (optional)

Mix with water to form soft dough.
Form into flattish palm-sized pieces.
Fry in generous amount of fat until golden brown, turning once to cook both sides.
Add fat as needed.
Serve hot—tastes like substantial doughnuts.

The First Klondike Baby

by Mary Carey

hat was it, Bill," said Dave, "that old Brownlow of the Fourth Form recited to us every Christmas? I know—
"It was the winter wild
When the Heaven born child,
All meanly wrapt,
In a rude manger lay."

"Why! don't you remember those pages of Milton he used to spout at us?" replied Bill.

"That was a great Christmas when our kids were ill and your mater asked me to Lincoln with you. Remember the star at the top of your Christmas tree, eh, Bill?"

"I wonder what they are doing there now," said Bill, with a sigh.

Johnny, who was busy steering the sled with a gee-pole, turned to the other two, saying, "If you fellows don't stop talking about Christmas and help with the dogs, it will be your last Christmas."

For the dogs were stumbling under the weight of the heavy load. The long run to Dawson and back, for supplies, had used up the strength of the sturdiest husky team on Eldorado Creek.

It was Christmas Eve in the Klondike, a clear, crisp night, with the Northern Lights darting across the sky and the stars twinkling through the quivering flashes of light. The three men were trudging along with their dog team to their cabin at Number Eleven Eldorado Creek. The cold was bitter—50 degrees below zero.

"We'll help in a minute, Johnny," said Bill. "But anyway, Dave, neither Palestine nor England has anything on the Klondike for stars! Look at that one over there. It is leading us on!" and Bill pointed with his fur-mittened hand to a particular star shining down on them with an almost benign and holy light.

"Well, you'll be frozen stiff beside the poor dogs if you two do not stop discussing stars and help with the load," returned the practical Johnny. "You must push behind while I steer, or the sled will upset. I'll attach the harness and help pull while you both shove."

Johnny attached the harness of the gee-pole over his shoulders with a strap across his breast and Bill and Dave went to the back of the sled. Just as Johnny was about to give the word to start, he suddenly stopped and listened. A low, moaning sound was heard on the still winter night.

"What's that, boys?" he asked.

"The wind," said Dave.

"A malemute pup," said Bill. "Poor little brute sounds as if something were wrong."

"Well, there's a very dim light over there," said Johnny.

"That's an old disused cabin; nobody lives in it, and it has no windows," said Dave.

"Yes, it has a window," said Bill. "One of those old gin bottle things stuck in the mud and moss."

"Anyway, there's no gol-darned sense to a light there tonight," replied Johnny. "And we had better investigate." The low, wailing sound was again borne to them over the frozen snow.

The three men left the dog team and tramped over the snow in the direction from which the sound had come. Here was a cabin, with a dim light shining through the window, and issuing from it at intervals were moaning notes of pain which now seemed to be mingled with a feeble wailing.

"Some dogs have got in here, I suppose," said Johnny.

"Oh, yes!" said Bill. "Dogs are so apt to have a light."

"Perhaps it is the reflection of your star shining," said Johnny, as reaching the cabin first, he pulled the door open.

"My God, boys!" he said as he staggered back. "It's a woman with a new born baby, all alone.... Bill, run to the sled and get that bottle of brandy we bought! You, Dave, come in with me."

The two of them stepped softly into the cabin and over to the bunk where a young girl lay with a drawn white face and deep purple circles already forming under the eyes and around the mouth. She made a feeble movement with her hand, and Johnny, bending down, took it tenderly in both his warm ones and gently chafed it.

Dave made up the fire in the stove and went out of the door to get some snow to melt for hot water. In the winter Eldorado Creek freezes solid and no water can be obtained except by melting snow.

The moaning of the mother had ceased with a long drawn out sigh and the hand dropped from Johnny's grasp, but the feeble wailing of the infant continued.

"God! What are we going to do?" said Johnny as Dave and Bill came to his side with the brandy, some of which they tried to force through the clenched teeth of the poor, young, hurt thing lying on the bed. Johnny was trembling all over, when Dave, with the perspiration standing out on his forehead, stepped forward.

"We must do the best we can for the poor little beggar," he said decisively. "Give us your jack-knife, Johnny… and perhaps the star that led us here will show me what to do."

Bill, who had just had a present from the Old Land of some soft woolen underwear, undressing, took off his shirt. It was the best thing in which to wrap the trifle of Klondike humanity, thrust suddenly into a literally cold, if not cruel world.

"It's a girl child," said Dave softly, when he had wrapped the little shivering body in Bill's warm undershirt.

"What in the name of God are we three to do?" asked Johnny after reverently covering the body of the young girl mother with an old blanket. He sat down on the stump of a tree which served as a chair in the cabin, looking at the other two, in utter dismay. Dave was awkwardly holding the baby, which, soothed by the warmth, had ceased its pitiful wailing.

"There's someone coming outside now!" said Bill. "It sounds as if it were a team of dogs. I can hear the runners on the snow."

In the next minute the door burst open and a young man dashed into the room.

"Here I am, Jen, old girl!" he called out. "I met the Mounted Police Doctor on the way up Bonanza. He'll take care of you, my dear."

Then he started back when he saw the three men. The baby began to cry feebly. Then, rushing to the bunk, pulling away the blanket, he saw the still form there, and with a moan, sank on the floor.

The Doctor of the Northwest Mounted Police stepped into the cabin, then quickly over to the quiet form. He looked at the young mother, tried to find the pulse and listened for the heart beats. Straightening himself with a shake of his head, he came over to Dave, took the baby from his arms and asked hurried questions of the three men.

The Doctor told how he had met the young man almost distracted on Bonanza Creek, where he had been to attend a case of accident. The tale was like so many others in the Klondike. This boy and girl from the Middle West, after reading the glowing accounts of the great discovery had decided to follow the gold rush. They married and started off on the adventure. Between them they had enough money to get to Skagway and from there on it had required the strength and endurance of strong bodies and strong souls to win out, which combination neither of them had. They had drifted from one place and one job to another till at last Jennie was taken ill and the young husband, able to work but little in the Arctic climate, had no place but the deserted cabin on Eldorado Creek where they could find a temporary shelter in order that their child might be born.

"I'll take charge here and attend to this poor young fellow who is half sick himself," said the Doctor. "We can take him back to Dawson to the barracks, but what can be done with the baby? It is too long a drive, fifteen miles. The child would die from the exposure at fifty degrees below." All this time he had been attending to the needs of the little mite.

"Where do you boys live?" he asked.

"About a mile farther up the Creek, at Number Eleven," answered Johnny.

"Any women about?"

"No, but there are a number of women on Eldorado and Bonanza Creeks, about sixteen," said Bill.

"Can you get any of them tonight?"

"Don't think so."

"Well, you fellows will just have to take care of the poor little wretch yourselves. I'll write out some directions for you."

And the Doctor sat down and wrote out instructions.

"You might put two or three drops of brandy in with the tinned milk and hot water as a stimulant, and give the child a few spoonfuls every three hours. The poor little thing has not much chance of life. Can you manage?"

"Yes," stoutly answered Bill. "I fed one of the nippers at home when he was ill once and I think that I can look after this baby."

"Well, find something to wrap the baby in, and if ever you got speed out of those dogs do it now. I'll come in the morning to see you, and attend to matters here." And the doctor turned to the bunk and the limp figure lying beside it.

They found some of the mother's clothes hanging on the wall and these, very awkwardly, they wrapped around the baby. Bill went out and got some blankets he had just bought in Dawson and, after warming them by the stove, put them in an old packing box which he had picked up in the cabin, placed the baby in the box and drew the blankets carefully over. This he carried out and fastened on the least exposed part of the load. Then, with Johnny and Dave helping the dogs to pull, while Bill walked behind guarding the box, they started on the run for their own cabin. Never had so strange a load gone along the Eldorado trail, or any other trail for that matter, as went that Christmas Eve—the dog team, the three men, and the baby, while the northern stars shone brightly on their pathway.

At the cabin of these three strapping "nurses," the fire was quickly lighted and the baby, still sleeping, was carefully laid on one of the home-made cots. Soon water was boiling and, following the Doctor's directions, Bill prepared the baby's food.

Meantime Dave and Johnny had cooked the supper to which they all drew up their stools. Just as they were finishing the baby gave a little cry, so Bill, having her food in an old tin cup on the stove, took her up while Johnny and Dave cleared away the supper dishes—three tin cups, three tin plates, and the frying pan—from which they all had helped themselves.

"I'll take the first shift," said Bill, who had constituted himself "shift boss."

Johnny fetched a new candle and stuck it in the candle stick, an empty beer bottle, and then he and Dave went over to the beds at the side of the room and were soon asleep.

Bill, having lulled the little creature, who now seemed quite contented and happy, was walking up and down with her in his arms, softly humming to himself one of the old Christmas carols brought to his mind by the unusual, yet strangely beautiful incidents of the night. It seemed almost as if he heard again the chimes of the old Cathedral at home pealing out the sacred Christmas hymns. "Silent Night, Holy Night." The old Christmas story had come anew to the three men that night on the lonely winter trail in the far-off Klondike. If the candle light was blurred for moments, who could wonder.

The next morning, Dave harnessed the dogs and was ready to gather in the women of the Creek, in order to find someone who would volunteer to care for their baby. By this time she was their own baby and they had appointed themselves her guardians.

"You boys be all ready when the women arrive, and a lot of the fellows will be coming along just to see The Kid," said Dave proudly, as he drew on his mittens and cap.

Johnny had tidied up the cabin and Bill, still chief nurse, was putting down the sleeping baby when the women, all excited by the news, began pouring into the cabin, each one eagerly offering to take the child. The mother heart of each woman beat softly for that little motherless one, even if it should mean added work to her household. Every one of them wanted the baby.

Bill, Dave and Johnny sat in judgment, listening to each woman's claim.

"What were you in the 'outside'?" asked Dave of each while the other two listened gravely to the answers.

"I was a cook in a hotel," said one, and another,

"I was a dressmaker."

"A school teacher."

"I was a stenographer."

And on they went, asking questions like three wise judges and weighing carefully the special qualifications which each woman seemed to have.

They had questioned about ten of them when an older woman shoved forward, saying,

"I minded my own business and looked afer my husband in the 'outside' and was not spending my time answering impudent questions from young idiots like you three. Hand that poor little innocent to me and you boys get busy and collect the 'dust' to buy milk for her."

She walked over to the bed and picked up the baby with wise, motherly hands. Many of them knew of the little grave she had left in distant Nova Scotia, and all conceded her natural right to have the baby.

It did not take long to collect the money from the men who had been arriving all the time in the cabin until it was packed to the door. One man after another, drawing out his "poke" of gold dust emptied part of it into the dish that Johnny was passing round. Dave brought out the scales and found that they had 25 ounces of gold dust, current value $400.00. Fresh cow's milk was $2.00 a pint and very scarce at that. Soon things were settled and Mrs. Brown, who worked the next claim with her husband, was escorted back to her cabin where she quickly had the child in more comfortable baby clothes that she hurriedly improvised.

When the Northwest Mounted Police's Doctor arrived, he reported the child's father very ill with pleurisy. If he recovered, he would be sent to his home.

And so the Christmas baby grew under Mrs. Brown's motherly care and was the pet of Eldorado Creek, though Johnny, Dave and Bill oversaw particularly her care and what they called her "education."

And so she grew fat and happy and was the pet of all Eldorado.

In the Spring, just before the "clean-up" on the claims, one day Bill said to Dave, —

"Say, the mater would have a fit if that child were not baptized."

"Well, why can't she be baptized?" said Dave. "I'd like to know. The weather is warmer and we could get away to Dawson before the 'clean-up' begins. Let's take her into Dawson next Sunday to the parson there."

So it was that after a great deal of fuss and consultation, in which almost every man and woman on the Creek joined, they all decided to go to Dawson the following Sunday. What would the baby be called? All sorts of fancy names were suggested such as Ruth, Marjorie, Myrtle, Gwendolyn, Dorothy and Muriel, but these were discarded as unfitting. Then plain names, Jane, Martha, Sarah, Ann, Katherine, Mary, but none could be agreed on.

"She must have a Klondike name," said Dave. "Real Klondike."

"What's the matter with Bonanza?" said someone.

"You darned idiots," said Mrs. Brown. "Fasten such a name on my wee lamb. I won't have it."

"Anyway it has got to be Eldorado," declared someone. "For she was the first baby born on the Creek."

Bill, after a few minutes of quiet thought, looked up.

"How about 'Edna Eldorado'?" he asked.

"That's it!" shouted the others. "'Edna Eldorado' she is and shall be."

Sunday dawned bright and fair. Early morning and all Eldorado Creek was astir, for was not the baby of the camp to be christened? Such a procession as there was, and how it grew as it passed through the little town of the Forks and went up Bonanza Creek to Dawson. Nor could the little Presbyterian log church in Dawson hold the people who crowded to see the "dedication" of the first Klondike baby.

Johnny, Dave and Bill, carefully shaved and in their best "outside" clothes, stood with the baby in front of the Communion Table, and when the parson took the little thing in his arms, held it up so that all in the church

could see the little fluffy golden head and said solemnly, "Edna Eldorado, I baptize thee," there were few dry eyes in the church, for the story of the child was known to them all and of how Bill, Dave and Johnny had been led by the Christmas star to "the place where the young child lay."

Magazine Editor's note:
Suggestive of "The Luck of Roaring Camp" by Bret Harte, yet in what one might call a sweeter mood, the accompanying story of "The First Klondike Baby" comes to "GOLD" from the pen of the wife of an eminent Canadian explorer and geologist. While she prefers to write with a nom de plume, it may be said that the writer was with her husband in the Klondike at the time of the incidents described and her small daughter with her—the first white child to go into Dawson City. There they lived and came to know of "Edna Eldorado"—Christmas Eve darling of the Klondike, born beneath the northern lights under tragic yet, in one sense, such "redeeming" circumstances.

The three men of the story were partners on "Number 11 Eldorado Creek." One was John Lind, now general manager of the St. Mary's Cement Company, the second was Skiffington Mitchell, an Englishman, and the third, William Wilkinson, nephew of Gen. Wilkinson. The story is told as a narrative, without appeal to the emotions, yet "GOLD" believes it to be one of the most beautiful of Christmas stories—an old-fashioned Christmas story which one might be glad to read to the children on the night of nights, as a page from the lives of the hardy men and fine women who made our Yukon history, and the saving of one little new life, almost by destiny, it would seem. And…we can't help wondering what became of little "Edna Eldorado"—the tiny heroine of the tale. Wouldn't it be a charming climax to find where she is today?

From *Gold Magazine*, 1933.
Another version of this story appears in the book *I Was There* by Edith Tyrrell, published in 1938. Mrs. Tyrrell was the wife of Joseph B. Tyrrell, a well-known geologist, and was with her husband in the Klondike at the turn of the century. Mary Carey was Mrs. Tyrrell's nom de plume in this *Gold Magazine* article. Edna Eldorado's story was long believed to be true, partly because of the specifics about the rescuers at the end of the story. Years later a letter from Ms. Carey to Johnny Lind, one of the supposed rescuers, was found in the Thomas Fisher Library, at the University of Toronto. In it she apologizes for using his name to lend authenticity to this fiction. The first non-native child born in the Klondike was Dawson Klondyke Schultz, born in 1897.

The Trapper's Christmas Eve

by Robert Service

It's mighty lonesome-like and drear.
Above the Wild the moon rides high,
And shows up sharp and needle-clear
The emptiness of earth and sky;
No happy homes with love a-glow;
No Santa Claus to make believe;
Just snow and snow, and then more snow;
It's Christmas Eve, it's Christmas Eve.

And here am I where all things end,
And Undesirables are hurled;
A poor old man without a friend,
Forgot and dead to all the world;
Clean out of sight and out of mind...
Well, maybe it is better so;
We all in life our level find,
And mine, I guess, is pretty low.

Yet as I sit with pipe alight
Beside the cabin-fire, it's queer
This mind of mine must take to-night
The backward trail of fifty year.
The school-house and the Christmas tree;
The children with their cheeks a-glow;
Two bright blue eyes that smile on me...
Just half a century ago.

Again (it's maybe forty years),
With faith and trust almost divine,
These same blue eyes, abrim with tears,
Through depths of love look into mine.
A parting, tender, soft and low,
With arms that cling and lips that cleave...
Ah me! it's all so long ago,
Yet seems so sweet this Christmas Eve.

Just thirty years ago, again...
We say a bitter last good-bye;
Our lips are white with wrath and pain;
Our little children cling and cry.
Whose was the fault? it matters not,
For man and woman both deceive;
It's buried now and all forgot,
Forgiven, too, this Christmas Eve.

And she (God pity me) is dead;
Our children men and women grown,
I like to think that they are wed,
With little children of their own,
That crowd around their Christmas tree...
I would not ever have them grieve,
Or shed a single tear for me,
To mar their joy this Christmas Eve.

Stripped to the buff and gaunt and still
Lies all the land in grim distress.
Like lost souls wailing, long and shrill,
A wolf-howl cleaves the emptiness.
Then hushed as Death is everything.
The moon rides haggard and forlorn...
"O hark the herald angels sing!"
God bless all men—it's Christmas morn.

From *The Collected Poems of Robert Service.*
   The Bard of the Yukon, Robert Service, came to Canada from his native England in 1896, but it was not until 1904 that he arrived in the Yukon. He worked as a bank clerk in Whitehorse and then at Dawson before devoting his energy to writing full-time. He left the Yukon in 1912, wandered the world and finally settled in France. His tiny cabin in Dawson is a much-visited tourist attraction.

Norwegian Miners

by Carl Lokke

The ten Monitors at the headquarters cabin on Stewart Island enjoyed a three-day celebration of Christmas, beginning on Saturday, December 24. That day some snow fell and the temperature stood at 5 degrees below zero. At 1:30 in the afternoon, however, the sun broke through the heavy clouds and the men saw a "beautiful golden reflection." Skog describes in his diary preliminary preparations for the holiday festivities.

> This morning we started to celebrate Christmas by opening a can of strong butter. This p.m. Matt Carlson presented us with a fine fruit cake which he brought from home last winter. We anticipate a fine Xmas dinner. We are all slicking up for Xmas. Gunderson has capped the climax by putting on a white "biled" shirt, standup collar, black necktie and sky blue suspenders. Doll made doughnuts, rice pudding and some tempting pies which he says we can sample tomorrow. He has no roller to roll out the crust so we had to use an empty whisky bottle.

At four o'clock the celebration of Christmas Eve began with a drink of whisky. At the supper table, the men talked of home and what people were doing there at Christmas time.

The temperature on December 25 stood at 11 below under cloudy skies. Doll produced a bottle of whisky and each man took a drink. For breakfast they had oatmeal with milk and sugar, and bread and butter and cheese—a good substantial start for a day of hearty eating. Skog was delighted with the noon dinner.

> At last the time arrived, and this is what our good cook Mr. Doll set before us to tickle our palates. First there was some very fine meat balls with onions, with this went bread, butter and cheese, then came tea with two doughnuts for each, then we had apple pie, this was not affectionate pie as it was about two in.

thick. The last was the very best of all. It was an excellent rice pudding with lots of raisins, this was covered with brandy sauce making the finest dish I have had since I left home.

The feasting continued at supper, a meal also highly praised by the diarist: *"We had an evening lunch consisting of fruit sauce, doughnuts, and a piece of Mrs. Carlson's fruit cake, made last February and brought over Chilkoot Pass. It was delicious. These things are appreciated by a man who lives on pork and beans the rest of the year."*

Entertainment followed the feasting. Visitors—Jay Johnson, Shuster, Sjostad, and Carlson—came in and helped arrange a varied program. Shuster sang a baritone solo, and Skog recited a poem, "The Dawson City Mining Man," followed as an encore by Mark Antony's funeral oration. Applause greeted Wold's execution of a *Polskdans* (rustic dance). First a quartet harmonized on some comic songs; next everyone joined in group singing led by Sjostad and Carlson; then lustily the men roared out popular songs,

Two men check the gold content of some gravel in the warmth of their cabin.

hymns, and national airs. The program lasted until bedtime at 11:30 p.m. It was about 15 below as the guests left the cabin for their own lodgings....

This evening's fun ended the Christmas festivities at headquarters—a happy interlude between months of hard work and more of the same to come. Somewhat the same feeling settled over the five miners still on Black Hills during this Christmas weekend: their strenuous efforts had produced nothing, and there was little prospect that their luck would change. They were on the losing end of a stampede and they knew it. Still, Christmas was Christmas and they observed the holiday with good food—special for the occasion—and such diversions as were readily available.

It snowed all day on December 24, Christmas Eve. The men put on clean clothing and ate with gusto a substantial meal served by Petersen, their efficient cook. *"We had a feast of beef* [moose] *steak and potatoes, biscuits, tea, fruit sauce, and rice pudding,"* wrote Clausen, echoing what was in the minds of his four partners: each was thinking of the celebrations at home.

Christmas Day at No. 153 on Black Hills was quiet. *"There is nowhere to go,"* Clausen wrote in his diary, *"nothing to see and nothing to hear—except our little dogs barking now and then."* The snow had ceased and the men stepped outside for a little target practice with revolvers. Erwin brightened the scene inside by making *"a good Alcohol punch, a very surprising thing to get up here."* He had kept for just this occasion a little bottle of spirits that he had bought in Seattle eleven months before. In the evening, Karlstrom, a native of Stockholm, played the mouth organ and the miners hopped about in a lively dance.

From *Klondike Saga*.

The members of the Monitor Company of Minnesota were a group of sixteen young Scandinavians, mostly Norwegians, who immigrated to the United States and joined the rush to the Klondike. They set up operations on Black Hills Creek, about sixty miles south of the Klondike, in the Stewart River country. Letters and diaries chronicle their adventures and dreams of gold. The results on Black Hills were disappointing and they left after about eighteen months. Many settled in the Pacific Northwest.

Northern Game

by Jeremiah Lynch

n December 21 the sun rose at ten and set at two; thermometer 45 degrees below zero. Withal, the stars were so bright, and the ice and snow so clear in the transparent atmosphere, that it was quite as easy to travel by night as by day.

On Christmas night a party of us dined at the principal restaurant. The dinner included moose, caribou, and ptarmigan. The moose and caribou were killed up the Klondike, east of Dawson, in the recesses of the Rocky Mountains, where large herds roamed. The hunters sledded the meat on dog-sleds down the Klondike, and sold it in Dawson at half a dollar per pound—the same price as frozen beef. The game meat was hard and close, and did not taste so well as the frozen beef from the "outside," which seemed far the better. It was odd to walk round Dawson and see carcasses of moose and caribou hanging side by side with carcasses of sheep and cattle. The price was uniformly the same. Ptarmigan, lovely in their snowy plumage, were shot even in the environs of Dawson, and especially up the Klondike. They made a delicious roast with dressing, and were numerous.

Boiled Moose Heart

Boil heart in water;
add onion, sage, salt and pepper.
Cook slowly until tender.

Moose Steak

Pound steaks well.
Dredge in flour; season to taste; and fry in grease with plenty of sliced onion. If the steak is not young, marinate steak in milk for 12–24 hours; this will tenderize it, and reduce strong flavors. Powdered milk or evaporated milk may be used.

From *Three Years in the Klondike*.

An ex-senator from San Francisco, Jeremiah Lynch joined the rush to the gold fields not to find, but to invest in a gold mine. He went to the Klondike, explored the available options and became a popular man-about-town in Dawson. He bought a mine on Cheechako Hill and ran it successfully for two years before returning to California.

Dawson Mass

by Eudora Bundy Ferry

 he most coveted invitation of the whole winter was a card to the Midnight Mass on Christmas Eve at the Catholic church. It stood, white and impressive, a beacon high on the bluff along the river where it could be seen for miles, a monument to its builder, Father Judge, the first Catholic priest in Dawson, who had also established the Catholic hospital and school. Admission had to be by card because the church could not possibly hold all who wished to attend. Doug had been given cards for us and we planned to go.

That evening we felt as if it were indeed the middle of the night when church time approached. It had been dark for so many hours that the world seemed to be enfolded in the very depths of endless night and the sun only a dream forgotten.

Our cabin was on the street which led to the church, and since it was only about four feet from the living room wall to the sidewalk, we could hear the people walking up the hill long before we were ready to go ourselves. There was no other sound, as it was far too cold to talk. The footfalls crunching on the snow were soft and continuous as the silent procession passed our door.

We put on our wraps and stepped out into the night to join the long line of churchgoers. The sky scintillated with stars, myriad and low-hanging. The cold struck to our very marrow as we dug our chins into the fur of our collars and curled our shoulders forward instinctively to ward it off. We became one with the line of muffled figures trudging uphill. Never had we felt so remote from gaiety and the warmth of sunlight as at this moment, when the sun we had not seen for weeks was at its farthest southern reach. From our hilltop in the dark and cold, the world seemed to flow down and away from us in every direction. We stood, indeed, at the lonely top. Only the stars kept watch. The silence, which was a force in itself, was only emphasized by the mournful howls of the Malemutes on the hills beyond us as they lamented their exile from the sun.

Some need was in each soul that climbed the hill that night, something strong enough to call us from our warm houses to the rigors of that walk, something that the church symbolized. Whether it was light, or music, or companionship, or something infinitely deeper, it took us, each bringing his own exigency, to that door.

We reached the church, bulking amorphous in the dark, and entered, grateful for the warmth and dazzled by the lights, and found ourselves seats. The interior was simple and unimpressive, the walls of tongue-and-groove lumber, varnished, the altar conventional and simply decorated. I was not interested in the decorations, however; the congregation was the focus of my attention.

Within this sanctuary were Indians, poorly dressed; teamsters from the creeks, wearing rough mackinaws; miners in coonskin coats; fine ladies in Canadian mink and jewels; government employees; engineers; Royal Northwest Mounted Police in their scarlet coats; a saloonkeeper; a former dance-hall girl; a doctor who had come from nobody knew where, his past closed off like a book that has been destroyed; and ourselves, people who were young and observant and eager, the new life that had flooded Dawson with the coming of the big mining companies. Row upon row we sat, each with his own reason for coming.

From the choir loft at the back of the church the organ broke the stillness; and the service had begun. The chorus of the regular choir was augmented by two truly fine voices—that of Mrs. MacDougall, beautiful wife of the gold commissioner, who had been trained in eastern Canada and in Europe, and that of Charles MacPherson, dominion land surveyor for our company, who possessed a full baritone. Several violins accompanied the organ. Never had the great traditional music of the church been given to a more appreciative audience or amid more striking incongruities, the development of the religious and musical tradition of a highly cultivated environment being poured out into an atmosphere both crude and remote. It found ready reception there and transported its listeners to the Bethlehem scene, equally remote and of like simplicity.

In the pauses between the words of the priest and the musical parts of the service, we could hear plainly the ululations of the Malemutes on the hills.

The last note was sung, the spell broken. We were dismissed, bemused by the deep sense of Christmas that possessed us. There was no talk, no laughter, as we filed out, felt again the impact of the cold, made our way down the hill.

Spirited Celebrations

by E.C. Trelawney-Ansell

Christmas Eve I was in the Monte Carlo—saloon and gambling palace—and it was a blaze of light, with everyone in good spirits, broke or otherwise. Sourdoughs and newcomers from all the creeks round crowded the bar, keeping the booze-knights and dust-weighers busier than they had ever been before. Every miner there with a full poke—or empty—was having a good time and "hitting it up." Those with rich claims never drank without the order, "Set 'em up for the 'house.' Drink on me, boys." This usually meant a round which would cost $200 or more. Good-hearted hilarity was the order of the night. Music from the dance hall at the end of the great room filled the air, as the piano and violin played a waltz or two-step.

Above all could be heard the voice of the dance-speeler as the miners went into their favourite square dance:

"Allermen left, bow to yer dames.

"Swing yer girl high.

"Now der chain, chassey and all to yer corners. And the next is a long, slow, dreamy waltz, gents.

"Don't be backward in coming forward. Take a look at these gay pea-hens and then grab one."

All this would be blended with a series of minor sounds, such as the soft slithering shuffle of muk-luks or moccasins on the sandy floor: the clink and tinkle of glasses, the popping of corks, the rustle of silk petticoats of the dance-hall girls, and their shrieks as some miner whirled them head-high in a square dance: the purr and rattle of the roulette wheels and the clinking rattle of the dice in the crap games.

From *I Followed Gold*.

When he was fifteen, Trelawney-Ansell set off for South Africa from his home in England. In 1896, he travelled to Canada to visit an uncle in Nanaimo, B.C., but quickly became restless and accompanied a prospector acquaintance to the Stikine area where they met some native people who wanted flour and offered gold nuggets in exchange. Unable to discover where the nuggets came from, the partners wandered north to the Klondike. Trelawney-Ansell eventually left the Klondike for Europe and then the gold fields of California.

Christmas Marketing on the Yukon

by Samuel Hubbard, Jr.

n the winter of '98 at a brand-new mining camp on the Yukon there was a select society. One dark afternoon just before Christmas, with the mercury standing below the zero mark at twenty some odd, and a bitter wind sweeping down the river, the Host blew into the cozy office of the Agent. The lamps were lighted and a big box stove was doing a brisk business with large sticks of dry birch wood.

The Host stood with his back to the stove absorbing the genial warmth and began in his abrupt way:

"I want you to do two things for me."

"All right," said the Agent, with ready courtesy, "what do you lack?" The Agent was used to doing things for people, but aside from that there was a budding friendship between these two.

"In the first place," said the Host, "I want you to take Christmas dinner with me."

"That's easy," said the Agent.

"In the second place, I want you to help me out with the dinner."

"Take the whole house if you want it," said the Agent, with a comprehensive sweep of his arm.

"No, I don't quite want the house," said the Host, "but I want that little Frenchman, your cook—what's his name?"

"Louis is yours," said the Agent.

"And I want a whole lot of other things," said the Host, with a sigh. "I'm afraid I'm up against it hard."

"What's the game?" said the Agent, becoming interested.

"Well, you see, it's this way," said the Host. "I've invited the Governor and his son, and the General and his wife, and you and I make up the party. Further, I have asked each guest to choose some dish he would like for dinner and however difficult I have agreed to provide it."

"Well, I admire your nerve," said the Agent, "you must imagine that San

Francisco or New Orleans is just around the next bend in the river. Do you know what the word Yukon means?"

"No," said the Host, despondently.

"It means, 'Nothing to eat,' and I want to tell you," said the Agent with conviction, "that it's infernally well named."

"Before we go any further," said the Host, entirely ignoring the Agent's triumph, "what is yours?"

"Rum omelette," said the Agent, without a moment's hesitation.

"Hum!" mused the Host, "rum of course, but that means fresh eggs with nothing but scrambled eggs in the town. Canned eggs won't omelette; I've tried 'em."

"Blackie's got a hen," suggested the Agent; "she roosts on the foot of his bed to keep from freezing to death."

"Yes, I know," said the Host, "but she laid her last egg on the steamer just before it reached town. No hope at all there."

"He's up against the real thing now," sang the Agent with delight. "By the way, what did the others choose?"

"To begin with the easiest, the Governor's son wants some dish cooked in the French fashion."

"Why not let Louis make a caribou sauté?" suggested the Agent.

"Just the thing," said the Host, cheering up.

"What next?"

"The General's wife wants fresh potatoes. No evaporated or granulated spuds go."

"Got any?" asked the Host anxiously.

"Frozen ones," said the Agent.

"Will they do boiled?"

"No, mashed," said the Agent, "whip 'em up with a little butter and canned cream and then brown 'em in the oven."

"Bully," said the Host, lapsing into the vernacular of the west and rubbing his hands together.

"What does the Governor want?" asked the Agent.

"Marrow on toast," said the Host dubiously.

"Holy smoke!" exclaimed the Agent. "Not a cow brute this side of Dawson and that is seven hundred and seventy-five miles and a quarter up the Yukon. Better start an air-ship for Seattle at once. There are two horses in town, you might buy one and—hold on a minute," as the dawn of an idea appeared in his eyes, "wait 'til I go out and look on the roof of the cabin." He stepped out of the door and returned in a few moments looking mysteriously triumphant.

"What's on the roof of your cabin?" asked the Host skeptically.

The Agent tip-toed dramatically up to him, put his hand to his mouth and said in a loud stage whisper, "moose shanks."

"What?" said the Host.

"Frozen moose bones full of marrow," explained the Agent, beaming. "You see I have had several moose hams this fall and as fast as the meat was cut off Louis threw them on the roof of the cabin intending to make soup for the dogs. Now what will be the dogs' loss will be the Governor's gain, for those bones are full of marrow, every one of them."

"Shake," said the Host as he extended his right hand.

"Now let's see," said the Agent musing, "what's next? Oh, yes, the General. Bet you the drinks I know what he wants! He wants booze."

"You're not so much," said the Host, laughing. "I guessed that myself. When I asked him, he put the whole proposition in as few words as possible; all he said was, 'lashin's o' champagne'."

"That means plenty, I suppose," said the Agent.

"Of course; got any?"

"Field's extra dry, seventy-five dollars a case," replied the Agent in his most business-like tone.

"Send up two cases," drawled the Host as though he was ordering half a dozen bottles of beer.

"Now," said the Host briskly, "these matters being settled, how about eggs?"

"There are the suicide's eggs," murmured the Agent.

"What," said the Host incredulously, "did that man who hanged himself with a wire from a beam in his cabin have fresh eggs?"

"Why, didn't you know," said the Agent with surprise, "it was brooding on eighteen thousand eggs that caused him to commit suicide. He thought they were all bad, you see."

"I should think," said the Host with conviction, "that brooding on eighteen thousand bad eggs would cause any man to lay violent hands on himself—even a Dutchman."

"But they weren't all bad, only he didn't find it out until after he was dead," protested the Agent with a grin. "I was a member of the coroner's jury that sat on the case, and when we investigated the effects of deceased we found sixteen barrels of fresh eggs worth two dollars a dozen. We therefore made a finding that deceased came to his death through failure to open one more barrel of eggs. See?"

"It reminds me," said the Agent reflectively, "of the Dutchman who sold his prospect shaft for fifty dollars. The purchaser sank one foot in the bottom of the shaft and struck it richer than Croesus. The Dutchman was mad as a March hare and swore that before he ever sold another mine he would go one foot deeper."

"Chestnuts," said the Host in a sarcastic tone.

"Let me tell you what to do when you go to buy your eggs," continued the Agent, not noticing the interruption. "Take a pocketful of money and a cold chisel and a hammer."

"What's all that for?" asked the Host with a show of interest.

"Well, you see the eggs are in lard, like holes in a cheese, and the lard is frozen solid as a rock. The Probate Court has charge of the matter and they sell the eggs for two dollars a dozen in the lard, purchaser's risk. You have to get 'em out yourself. If you get six whole eggs out of a dozen you are a dandy. They won't let you use a steam thawer because it would boil all the eggs. I want to tell you that the Probate Court of this town is strictly onto its job."

"Now," continued the Agent with decision, "in the language of me Grecian friend Herodotus, the Father of History, that's all I have to say about eggs."

"Is there anything else you want that you don't see?" asked the Agent after quite a pause.

"Yes," replied the Host, "I want roses. They are my choice. But in latitude 64 degrees north, and in the dead of an Arctic winter, one might as well wish for a chunk of Polaris."

"Oh, I don't know," said the Agent encouragingly, "how would a dozen 'Jacks' and a dozen American beauties do, with a few sprays of apple blossoms to lay on the table?"

"What's the use of trying to be funny," said the Host in an injured tone. "It's not in the least becoming."

"Well, I've got 'em just the same," said the Agent stoutly.

"With windows at five dollars a sash, I haven't noticed many greenhouses since I landed in town," said the Host with thinly veiled sarcasm.

The Agent made no reply to this but quietly stepped into the other room and returned presently with a birch-bark vase in each hand. One contained a large bunch of magnificent Jacque-minots and the other an equally handsome lot of American beauties.

"Well, I'll be—jiggered," said the Host, catching himself just in time, "you could knock me down with a feather."

"That's what they are," said the Agent complacently.

"What what are?" said the Host, thoroughly mystified.

"Feathers," said the Agent, indicating the roses with a nod of his head.

"Well, I'll be switched!" said the Host, forgetting himself completely, "if they are not feathers you can have my hat for a foot-ball. But so cleverly done that they look like the real thing."

"Spray a little perfume on 'em and after about two of the General's 'lashin's' nobody could tell 'em," said the Agent.

"Where did you get them?" asked the Host with interest.

"Oh!" said the Agent, who was inclined to be poetical, "they fluttered down from the wings of Aurora!"

"Fluttered down from the wings of geese," replied the Host, who was not in the least so.

"Well, they are goose feathers," admitted the Agent reluctantly, "but you needn't be so disgustingly matter of fact about it. Besides, I've got the apple blossoms upstairs in the store."

"Well if you don't beat the Dutch," said the Host glancing around, "what sort of joint is this anyway? Is this the ubiquitous Wanamaker's department store or what is it? From French cooks to American beauty feather roses and from champagne to marrow bones. It's a wonder to me that you don't have some of those flowers made up into a feather bed and then you would present the anomaly of a man in Alaska literally lying on a bed of roses—ha! ha! ha!"

"You think you're pretty funny, don't you?" said the Agent with disgust.

"I must be getting home," said the Host, worming himself awkwardly into his squirrel-skin parkie. "Dinner at six o'clock sharp, and don't forget to send up all the stuff, including Louis, the marrow bones and the roses. Good night," and off he went.

From *Sunset Magazine*.
  A fictional story by an American writer.

Fireside

by William Haskell

I heard of a Christmas celebration down the river which afforded a glimpse of the life of those who face the severe climate for something besides gold. The story was told by the wife of a man connected with the post in that locality.

The first Christmas she spent in the Yukon district had been two years before, when, with her husband, she lived in a log house at Fort Cudahy, about fifty miles below the mouth of the Klondike. There was but one other white woman there, but it was a comfortable little community, and the gold fever had not become epidemic. Two of her husband's bachelor friends were invited to spend Christmas Day, and she made extensive preparations for a feast that would be a real Christmas treat. Turkey? They do not wander around the Klondike waiting to be shot for Christmas tables. Mince pie and plum pudding? Not on the Yukon. The dinner consisted of a huge haunch of roasted bear meat cut from the carcass of an animal that had been killed

A log cabin is almost hidden under a winter's accumulation of snow.

hundreds of miles away, and they were glad enough to get even such meat. Bear meat is very much like roast pork, and, if tender, is quite a dainty dish when properly prepared.

They sat and talked all day with the wood blocks heaped up on the blazing hearth, and the rough log walls of the house reflecting cheerfully the light from the flames that danced and sparkled around the chimney corner. Outside it was a very cold, cold world. Christmas weather in the Klondike is not comfortable. The wind howled around the log house and the snow fell, steadily accumulating until it made a thick white covering that effectually kept any drafts from finding their way in. The thermometer outside registered fifty degrees below zero. But inside they were as cosy and warm as any eastern home heated by modern appliances could be, and in their quiet way, though many thousand miles from what they really called home, they enjoyed themselves and were happy. The men were certainly grateful for some homelike fireside to gather around on that Christmas day in the Yukon.

Bear Steak

The bear should be young and tender. One that has eaten blueberries is best.
Rub steak with onion and spread with grease; sprinkle with salt and pepper.
Broil in a hot oven, turning frequently, or fry over high heat.
Cook well.
Bear meat, like pork, should be handled carefully, and does not keep well.

Bear Roast

Put roast in pot with lid.
Add water to a depth of about 2 inches.
Sprinkle with salt and pepper.
Add onions. Simmer for about 2 1/2 hours for young bear, 4 hours for older animal.
Cook well.

From *Two Years in the Klondike and Alaskan Gold Fields*.
A restless young man from New England, William Haskell worked at many jobs, drifting westward. In Colorado he met a prospector who had just returned from Alaska. They became partners and journeyed to the Klondike, where they prospected successfully.

The Paystreak

Dawson City, Monday, December 25, 1899

he Paystreak, the official journal of the Bazaar held in behalf of St. Mary's hospital, extends greetings of this festive season to all its readers, and heartily welcomes to the Bazaar every citizen of Dawson, and every miner from the creeks.

The promoters of this function have aimed to accomplish a two-fold benevolence—that of giving a pleasant entertainment during Christmas week to the many far from home and home festivities—together with the greater purpose of gathering a substantial gift for the good sisters of St. Mary's hospital; to assist them in their work of ministering to the sick.

During the past year, our Territorial Council have come generously to the aid of the sick and destitute in the Yukon Territory, having appropriated some eighty thousand dollars for their relief—and this largely by contribution to the hospitals. And it is extremely gratifying to see their splendid effort supplemented and seconded by the public generally.

Benevolence is contagious. He who gives once will give again; and one of the strongest indications that Dawson has passed from the "camp" stage into the era of permanent growth is the recently evinced stirring of a public spirit—a recognition of a common humanity and citizenship.

The Bazaar committee desires to thank most cordially all those who have so kindly and generously responded to their appeal for assistance—the ladies who have worked so indefatigably, the gentlemen who have advised and aided them; and the merchants who have contributed, not once but repeatedly, meeting each fresh solicitation with kindly interest and prompt response. The work of soliciting contributions is at no time an agreeable one to those thus engaged; but in this instance it has been made a pleasure by the unvarying courtesy extended. Again and yet again the committee tender their thanks.

And now upon the public—the strong stirring public of this great mining camp by the river—rests the completion of the undertaking—by its presence and purchase, by hearty support and cordial good will to fill the Bazaar with cheer and its coffers with coin.

The *Paystreak* invites everyone to make of the pretty Fair a daily abiding place during the holiday week—to live here, laugh here, dine here, spend here—and in the midst of the merry fun and fascinations to revive the dear home associations of bygone days and far away.

A Merry Christmas, friends, and for the New Year A Rich Paystreak.

> I wish you a Merry Christmas
> And a Happy New Year
> A pocketful of money
> And a cellar full of beer.
> My feet are very dirty
> My shoes are very thin
> I've got a little pocket
> To put my money in.
>
> (Author unknown)

Faith Fenton was editor of *The Paystreak*. It promoted a Christmas bazaar to help raise funds for St. Mary's Hospital. The hospital, built by Father William Judge, the "Saint of Dawson," was deeply in debt when Father Judge died early in 1899, and the hospital was taken over by the Sisters of St. Ann.

Merry Christmas

Dawson, December 1898

 he Nugget extends to all its readers and friends in the city and on the creeks the wish for a happy and joyous Christmas. With most of us there will be a great many of the customary features lacking in the celebrations this year. Nevertheless, we can take pleasure in celebrating the joys of former years and look forward to similar occasions in the future when again old ties and friendships will be renewed.

Yet the Christmas season even on the Klondike will be filled with pleasurable events and if our advice is taken we are of the opinion that the recurrence of our greatest holiday in this year of our Lord 1898, will be an occasion long to be remembered. The best we can wish for our friends is a Merry Christmas, a prosperous season and a handsome clean-up in the spring.

> From *The Klondike Nugget.*
> *The Klondike Nugget* was the first newspaper published in Dawson, in May 1898. Circulation probably topped two thousand copies daily. *The Nugget* folded in July 1903.

Gold Bottom Christmas

Dawson City, December 26, 1897

My dear Mother:

I have looked and waited for a letter but have not received one since I got the one dated Aug. 29. A Christmas present of a letter from home would have been the best thing I could think of but alas! it did not come. They have been expecting the mail in every day of the last month but it has not arrived as yet and I expect that is the reason I have not heard. Well, I am located in a new place, No. 30 Below on Hunker Creek. I have a fine partner, his name is Joe Roberts from Montana. I brought the men from Live Rocks up with me and have them working for me now. The thermometer stood between 50 and 60 below all the time we were building the cabin but has moderated now to an average of 10 below. I suppose Father will laugh when I say that I was boss carpenter on the construction but

A winter camp on the trail to the Klondike.

Claim #24, Gold Bottom, North-West Territory, 1897 Christmas Dinner

GIVEN BY SINGLETON AND WAGNER.
IN HONOR OF THEIR FRIENDS

Mr. and Mrs. Boyaker, Fred Kellersman, Joe Roberts,
R.D. Menzie, Prof. J.O. Hall, William Welch, Mr. Bayne.

Soup: Rice Tomato.

Fish: Boiled King Salmon a La Wagner.

Entree: Rague of Rabbit a La Welch; Sausage a La Bayne;
   Macaroni and Cheese a La Menzie;
   Peach Cobbler Sauce a La Professor Hall.

Roasts: Moose—Cranberry Sauce;
   Pork—Sauce Robert's;
   Mutton a La Boyaker.

Vegetables: Mashed Potatoes; Stewed Tomatoes;
   Corn in Cream; Klondyke Strawberries.*

Dessert: Prune Pie; Apple Dumpling—Cream Sauce;
   Fruits and Cakes; Mrs. Crosse's Salem Fruit-Cake;
   Chocolate Cake; Bartlett Pears; White Cherries;
   American Cheese; Singleton's Confectionerys.

Drink: Green Tea; English Tea; Siwash Tea; Black Coffee.

Guests are requested to bring their dishes and their robes.
Dinner at Three P.M.

* * * * *

P.S. Plenty of dog feed on hand.

nevertheless I was. We have not struck anything very rich as yet but expect to make good wages out of this deal. Joe is running our lay and I bought in with a fellow named David Reirick who used to live in Richville just a little way west of Batavia. The ground lies right near ours so we can work it out very easy. The days are very short now, it being barely light enough to eat dinner without a candle. I suppose before this reaches you that one of the boys I came in with will have been to see you and told you all about the country. I send out a few small nuggets to give you some idea of the way they find it here. So many have had to go out on account of provisions and each one has a little to sell so it has left quite enough to supply all who are left. Outfits sell as high as $1.25 per pound including boxes and hardware. You would be surprised to see me make yeast bread and it is good. Joe and I were invited to Christmas dinner up on 24 Gold Bottom with the fellows who came in with us last spring, John Singleton and Earnest Wagner. I enclose the bill of fare. Dogs are as essential here as horses are on the outside and cost from $300 apiece so that accounts for the "PS" on the Bill of Fare. We had a fine dinner and a most enjoyable time coming home the next day. You spoke in your letter about my not getting some of the newspapers. I think I got them all at least I got quite a number and I tell you that they have been appreciated, read and reread dozens of times. I have loaned them to a great many and they all congratulate me on having someone thoughtful enough to send so many. During the summer they will bring them up the river on the boats in bundles but will not use the trail. Well, I must close.

With lots of love to all,
Bob

From *Klondike Gold* by Kenneth J. Kutz.
    This letter, one of many published in Kutz's *Klondike Gold*, is of unknown provenance, but was likely the R.D. Menzie listed on the "bill of fare." Therefore, sadly, nothing is known about Bob, or whether he realized his dreams of gold.
    *The Klondyke Strawberries on the menu is Yukon slang for beans.

Diary of Ebenezer McAdam

Sunday, December 25, 1898

Christmas here again. What a change in a year; 4,500 miles from home and not one cheering word for nine months. Where will we be 12 months hence? In this country? Will we meet with success during the next year? What I would give to see my two little darlings today. No doubt they are enjoying themselves and perhaps thinking of me.

All our toboggans are ready and we have decided to leave our shack permanently about the 15th of January. Ten loads are cached about 8 miles up—Andrew three, Henry and Charlie two each, and the rest of us one each. We will probably move our caches about 8 miles each move, with our camp

Stampeders preferred to travel in groups for company and safety.

midway between, so that at no time will we be more than 4 miles from camp. This we consider advisable in order to avoid danger, in the event of storms coming up suddenly.

We had a visit from the Indians a week ago. Ten dog teams came down with meat and all here will have a good Christmas dinner. We received a good share trading shirts, sweaters, tea, etc. for what we got. All teams returned loaded with supplies from the various parties here. We were foolish enough to allow several opportunities to pass but will try hard next time they come to send up 1,000 to 1,500 lbs. We took advantage, while the Indians were here, to engage two of them to carry the mail to McPherson and bring back any letters that may be there for us. All the citizens are now anxiously awaiting their return. They left the 22nd and we expect them back about the 15th of January. We raised $100 in cash and provided supplies for the round trip. I have ordered a pair of Loucheux snowshoes and a deer skin coat.

We had three meals today: breakfast at 7 a.m., dinner at 12 a.m. and supper at 6 p.m. Andrew brought out the plum cake made by his sister over a year ago, and it went fine:

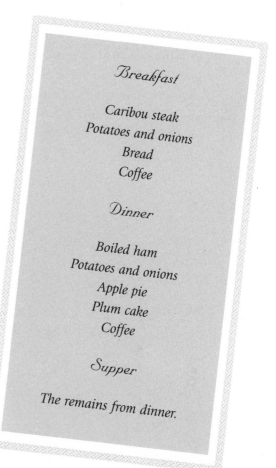

Breakfast

Caribou steak
Potatoes and onions
Bread
Coffee

Dinner

Boiled ham
Potatoes and onions
Apple pie
Plum cake
Coffee

Supper

The remains from dinner.

Monday, December 26, 1898

We did not get up till late as we did not go to bed till 2 a.m. Spent part of last evening at [George] Mitchell's shack and had a good drink, the first since I left Montreal. We had music and speeches. Did not remain late as Mr. McGruder from the lower shacks was here, and promised us a spiritualist meeting in the evening in our shack. It began about 9 p.m. and lasted till 1 a.m. Besides our own party, Dr. Brown, Dr. Sloan, Judge Morse and George Dalgeish were present; McGruder called our meeting a fairly successful one. The spirits spoke quite freely. I was the only one who did not converse. Each asked a number of questions relative to the health of family and friends, and also about our prospects in the gold fields. The answers received as regards our prospects were very satisfactory. Our party is to take out $1,500,000. The spirits also told us that the river at the head of this stream is the Stewart. Let us hope that what we heard has at least some truth in it. I am, so the spirits said, to receive seven letters and some photographs when the Indians return [as it turned out McAdam received no mail at all]. "What fools we mortals are."

We have been invited to the Huron shack for another spiritualist meeting this evening.

From *From Duck Lake to Dawson City: The Diary of Ebenezer McAdam's Journey to the Klondike: 1898–1899.*

Ebenezer McAdam, a Montrealer born in 1859, joined the rush to the Klondike. His search for gold was unsuccessful and in Dawson he became a clerk with the North American Transportation and Trading Company. Later he was promoted to resident manager of the company and was an upstanding citizen of Dawson. He remained in the Yukon until his death in May 1927. A widower, he left his two young daughters behind when he went North.

Moosehide Celebrations

by Laura Beatrice Berton

 few days before Christmas a few of us accompanied the Stringers on what was to become an annual trip to the Indian village of Moosehide around the big bluff downriver from Dawson. The party numbered about fifteen and we drove down on the river ice in the great North-West Mounted Police sleigh, drawn by a spanking pair of handsome blacks. As we swept along the frozen river road, the bishop told stories about his life among the Eskimos.

"I'll never forget the time at Old Crow when old Joe Adam insisted I'd named his daughter 'Gasoline'," he said. "I had an awful time of it until I could get back to the Mission church and look up the record. It was 'Kathleen', I'm thankful to say, but I doubt if Joe ever changed it."

The sleigh drew up at the little Indian church in Moosehide. The Indians were gathered inside and here we put on an amateur concert, I singing something that I considered appropriate, the bishop making a short speech in dialect, and Mrs. Stringer, dressed in beaded and fringed buckskin, singing "Jesus Loves Me" and "The Church's One Foundation" in Eskimo. This latter was an instant hit with the Indians, who insisted on several encores. This done, a member of the tribe named Happy Jack entered dressed as Santa Claus, and distributed presents.

The missionary at Moosehide, who arranged these festivities, was an Englishman who had been in the country for years. The Bird used to say that every man in the Yukon had at least one good novel locked up inside him, and I dare say that this quiet, drab little man, who lived all his life among the Indians, was no exception. I heard just enough of his story to be intrigued. He had come to Moosehide five years before the gold rush—before Dawson City existed. They were lonely years. Finally, the previous prelate, Bishop Bompas, a man of fixed determinations, arranged a marriage between him and a half-breed girl of the village. She had been deeply in love with a miner from the creeks, but her father and the bishop were insistent that she marry the missionary. This feudal arrangement was carried out without a great deal of enthusiasm from either partner, but now, looking at them, I could not detect the marks either of tragedy or of bliss on their features. They looked, in short, like any other married couple after the tenth year.

A few days after the Moosehide trip, with a great jangling of sleigh bells and a great swirl of powdered snow, the fast dog-teams of the Peel River Indians whisked into town on their annual pilgrimage down the Arctic Circle to Dawson. They were a dramatic and colourful group of natives. Their dogs were decorated with great pompoms of brightly coloured wool and their harnesses were alive with little bells. The men wore handsome caps bright with beads and the women wore intricate beaded shawls. They were magnificent-looking people, with long black hair of great sleekness, high foreheads, good noses, strong white teeth and a straight look in the eyes. They carried themselves with grace and dignity and did everything with a certain air. They wore jaunty buckskin jackets, heavy-beaded gauntlets and fur caps decorated with the tails of wild animals.

They were a clever, intelligent people [....] The women, I noticed, had an ingenious arrangement for carrying young children in beaded bags strapped to their backs. These bags were filled with fresh moss that served as a disposable diaper, and as they walked about town you could see the tiny faces with black alert eyes peeping out from within their snug cradles.

But they were child-like people, these Indians. They had come into town to trade, bearing flat bales of furs in their sleighs, which they sold to the Northern Commercial Company, whose store seemed like fairyland to them. Two things in particular intrigued them: electric-light bulbs and cameras. They bought dozens of globes to take back to their tents in the belief they would replace candles. As for cameras, they went about snapping at everybody and everything for all of their time in town.

Their sleighs were parked for the most part in a long line outside Bishop's House, and later in the week, before they again turned their faces north, Mrs. Stringer asked me to help at a Christmas dinner she was organizing for them. It was held in a log building off an alleyway near the church. Here the Indians sat at long tables eating bacon and beans and stewed moose and not saying a word. Their table manners were beautiful and I remarked on this to Mrs. Stringer in some surprise.

"Archdeacon McDonald's training," she said. "Don't forget he lived forty years among them."

After the moosemeat they were given beef, which was a great treat for them, and fabulous quantities of pie. I played some hymns on the little organ, to which they responded lustily in their own language, for the hymn book had also been translated by the indefatigable Archdeacon McDonald.

Because of my musical training I was in regular demand in Dawson for concerts and at other events. During one period, I played the organ in the Christian Science Church, then hurried over to St. Paul's to sing in the Anglican choir. On Christmas Eve, along with other choir members, I became a Roman Catholic. The R.C. choir was small and we always helped them out at their Midnight Mass, singing lustily in Latin as if we had been lifelong Papists. Usually, the Presbyterian choir came along, too, but the practise finally ceased when somebody counted noses and discovered that the Protestants far outnumbered the Romans.

Klondike Stew

Put some flour and seasonings in a bowl.
Cut up about 2 pounds of moose, bear, caribou or sheep into small pieces.
Roll in flour.
Brown lightly in grease in frying pan.
Put in pot with any seasonings, chopped onions or tomatoes, and one cup of water.
Simmer slowly for 2 hours. Can add chopped potatoes or rice. Add water if necessary.

From *I Married the Klondike*.
As a young Ontario school teacher in search of adventure, Laura Beatrice Berton came to the Yukon in 1907 to teach in Dawson for a year. She married and stayed for twenty-five years. She is the mother of author Pierre Berton.

Dawson Winter

by Faith Fenton

ecember has been as superb a winter month as one could wish, even in eastern Canada. Only once or twice throughout the entire month has the thermometer dropped to an uncomfortable degree of frigidity. In fact, since the bitter week of continuous 30 and 40 degrees below in mid-November we have had nothing until within the past two days that would not have been acceptable and timely weather in Ontario.

The temperature dropped on the day after Christmas, however, and at the present moment of writing on this last day of the year, ranges at the brisk point of 42 degrees below.

There is always a cloudiness or haze in the air on these very cold days. It is not the clear, brilliant sparkle and snap of the east. Whether it be due to the absence of sunlight or the vapor arising from this cluster of human habitation in the Klondike Valley, or from other reasons, I do not know, but the trees are draped with frost. It clings over the rough log cabins and touches them into beauty. Last night as I ran the few hundred yards that separates the cosy Victorian Order cabin from my own quarters the air was so weighted with whiteness that all the way was blinded and the trail difficult to keep. It was 47 degrees below zero, and all this shut-in valley world was hushed in an enveloping white haze, through which the cabin lights burned dimly, while the stars were altogether dimmed.

But there was no wind—we know little of wind in the Yukon Valley, and its absence makes 40 below quite possible, and 20 below comparatively mild. Yet I do not wish it to be inferred that the former temperature is comfortable. No one wishes to be out in the open longer than necessary. Water freezes in our rooms if removed any distance from the fire; our ink freezes; we eat frozen potatoes, and satisfy our longings for fresh fruit by eating frozen oranges thawed in water. It is not comfortable, but it is possible to live and get a fair amount of enjoyment out of life. Men travel over the river ice and find sufficient warmth in running with the dogs. Even many eager for claims and money-making trudge up and down the trails to El Dorado, Bonanza, Sulphur or Dominion, a distance of between twenty and thirty miles. Indeed, it appears to me that, if properly protected, women here stand the climate quite as well as the men.

Speaking from an experience up to this midwinter date, and without prejudice, my previous assertion may be confirmed that the Yukon winter is not one whit more formidable than that of Quebec, and in the matter of absence of wind preferable to the latter.

New Year's Eve

Christmas has come and gone, and we close our letter in the last hours of the year 1898. A light wind has lifted the haze from the valley, and all the still white scene of ice-blocked river, twinkling cabins and waved mountain tops is lit by a clear, round moon.

If it were not such an utterly phenomenal attitude in view of all the defamatory things that have been written and uttered concerning this Yukon country, the writer would confess to an appreciation that is growing perilously akin to fondness for this unique and picturesque mining camp.

From the *Toronto Globe*.
World interest in the Klondike was so high that the *Toronto Globe* sent Faith Fenton to Dawson as their special reporter. Fenton's dispatches described life in the Klondike and were eagerly awaited; this one concerns Christmas 1898.

St Paul's Church
Archival Records

A page from a Christmas card sent in 1902 to commemorate the new church.

The old log church, which did good service to the church people of Dawson from the autumn of 1897 to the summer of 1902, was built under the supervision of the first rector of the parish, Rev. R.J. Bowen, now of White Horse.

At first it consisted of the nave only and was used as a school-house as well as a church. In the spring of 1898 a chancel was added.

The Rev. H. A. Naylor, B.A., who succeeded Mr. Bowen in June, 1899, did not come as a stranger to Dawson; for it was he who had tramped the creeks in the summer of 1897, collecting money for the erection of the first church in Dawson. During his time the interior was renovated and made to present as church-like an appearance as was possible under the circumstances.

In March, 1902, the parishioners undertook to put up a new building and appointed a committee to collect the necessary funds. So well did this committee do its work that on June First the ground was excavated for the foundations and the new church ready for use by Aug. 9th. On that day the church people of Dawson had the joy of joining with their fellow-subjects throughout the Empire in celebrating the coronation of their Gracious Majesties, King Edward VII and Queen Alexandra, and also of opening the new St. Paul's to the service of God.

That we have such a handsome and suitable building in which to offer up our worship is, under the blessing of God, due to the untiring labours of the committee appointed to secure the necessary funds, to the response made by the church people of Dawson and their friends, and especially to the kind liberality of the Bishop of the Diocese and the Society for the Promotion of Christian Knowledge.

The church still lacks suitable furniture, but that we trust will be provided in due course.

James R.H. Warren.

Christmas Card, 1902

This gold nugget–ringed card records the dates of freeze-up on the Yukon River in the fall and when the ice started to move in the spring of 1899, 1900, 1901 and 1902. Once the river was frozen, Dawson City was virtually isolated until the spring. Bets were—and still are—made on the exact time and date the river ice goes out.

All dressed up for a men-only Christmas dinner.

First Christmas in Atlin City

by William White

Boxing Night '98
Atlin City, B.C.

My dear Lill (and all)

I have had you all in my thoughts during the last four or five days and had I been fool enough to mope and get homesick, I should have suffered a great deal by drawing too vivid a comparison between my present Christmas and that of last year. But resolutely determined to allow of no such tomfoolery, I have entered heart and soul into a plan for spending Christmas which has succeeded as only success can succeed. As I told you in my last letter the English boys in camp (about 40) decided to join in preparing, eating and digesting a Christmas Dinner that should be a credit to the dear old country we love so well. One never realises one's affection for the land of our birth until separated by 8000 miles or so. For the purpose of getting up this Dinner, a Committee of the Boys was formed, and your humble "little brodder" had the honour of being elected Secretary. For weeks preparations had been made for having as good a time as circumstances of our environment would permit, and amongst all residents of the "old sod" the watchword has been "Christmas of the good old sort in the good old way." But I had better start at the beginning and tell you how we kept Christmas in Atlin.

Christmas Eve was a beautiful night. The moon shone forth in the heavens with a lustre altogether unusual even in this country with its glorious atmosphere, whilst the snow underfoot was as crisp and dry as a well-cooked biscuit. At midnight seven of us repaired to Dr. Talbot's Drug Stores at the foot of Rant Avenue for the purpose of inaugurating the first Christmas in Atlin by singing a selection of carols in various parts of the town. Punctual to the minute we sallied forth and in a few minutes the beautiful hymn "Christians Awake" floated upward through the frosty air. Mr. Anderson, an American, and his young bride from sunny California, were evidently taken by surprise, but greatly appreciated the singing which was really of a very high order. As you know, I am no singer myself and my presence in the group was more that of a friend than a songster but my partner Williams is a grand alto and Dr. Talbot a good bass and the other four very fair singers indeed. At Mrs. Wright's we sang "Noel" and at Mr. and Mrs. Ogilvie's "Adeste Fidelis" and "Christians Awake." Here nothing would do but we must come in and have supper—hot coffee, cocoanut cake and real marmalade (Keillers). Our next visit was to the Atlin Hotel and here again we had to go inside and warm up. Williams and I being teetotal boys, accepted cigars instead of toddy. From here we went to Mr. and Mrs. Davis on 2nd Street and here again we found a big supply of coffee, cake and tarts awaiting us. But we had to refuse this time, for at this rate of progress we should never cover the city area. Opposite the Opera House (about the size of our Drill Hall) on Discovery Avenue we gave Mr. and Mrs. Kinney a couple of carols and in acknowledgement Mr. Kinney is presenting us with a box of 590 cigars, which are selling at 1/- each here now. Mr. and Mrs. Gregory from Australia were then visited and finally we called upon Mr. Jameson, and here were regaled with hot cocoa till we felt like bursting up altogether. Well as it was half past three we looked longingly towards our beds and soon our bodies followed our glances and we were sleeping contentedly in the arms of Morpheus.

On Christmas Day we were congratulated on all sides and by none more heartily than the Yankies, to whom carol singing came as a welcome novelty, as it appears that the Waits are almost unknown in the States.

Well Christmas Day was a busy day for me, and indeed for all on the committee, for we were determined that the Dinner should be a knock-out and indeed it was. I should like Father to have been there. He would have found it so novel and fresh. Each member had to bring his own knife, fork, spoon, plate and cup and a candle and as there were forty present we were able to have fifteen or twenty candles on the table at once, which brilliant illumination lighted up the cabin in grand style. The log house lent for the occasion was 20 × 20 and the walls were nicely decorated with guns, revolvers, greenery and the Canadian flag. At nine o'clock punctual, each man was in his seat and the excitement ran high when Dr. J.F. Phillip of Aberdeen took the chair. Now I think I had better give you a list of the various things we bought and which the ladies had kindly cooked and made into pies, puddings, stews etc. etc.

21 lbs Moose (an animal about the size of a large cow)
2 lbs Moose Tongue
4 lbs suet
8 grouse
2 rabbits
3 lbs bacon
1 lb salt pork
15 lbs potatoes
3 tins milk
40 lbs flour
6 lbs mince
10 lbs sugar
5 lbs butter
1 bottle celery salt
5 lbs cheese
3 boxes spices
9 lbs currants
5 lbs raisins
1 lb tea
1 lb coffee
2 tins marmalade
4 lbs prunes
4 lbs apples
1 cup molasses
half pint brandy
1 pt rum
2 dozen eggs
1 tin mustard
1 tin pepper

Now you can see that when these things are made into the various things, such as plum pudding, mince pies, cakes, stewed fruits etc., it must mean a meal vastly different to beans and bacon, almost our daily food for the last few months. Guess then our excitement as the great dinner drew nigh. Some of us hadn't eaten all day so that our appetites might be sharpened and that we might carry away as much of the good things as possible. Well Lill that dinner lasted 2 hours and a half. Two hours and a half of solid eating without a break, except to get wind, and one poor chap managed to get what he called his second wind and by jove it was terrible the tragic way in which that fellow started in on his second dinner. For the first hour of the dinner scarcely a sound could be heard save when some poor fellow heaved a sigh of contentment and happiness whilst pausing to get his plate replenished.

But such a state of things could not last forever and after eleven o'clock the intensity of purpose written on every face began to give place to a benign and self-complacent affability that soon became as hilarious and genial as only can be found in a John Bull party—after dinner, and the meal that began with a rigid silence ended amidst laughter and jollity that sounded as English as one could wish.

The men now retired to the Drug Stores for a chat and a smoke whilst the ladies sat down to their dinner, which by the way they well deserved, for it was no mean task to keep forty hungry men supplied for 2 and a half hours. Meanwhile I installed myself as head cook and bottle washer and washed and wiped all the plates, cups and knives, forks, spoons etc. By the way I had forgotten to mention that I wore my best black coat for the occasion—the first time since leaving Vancouver. It was a treat to feel that I looked respectable again and if I had only a collar with me I should have been in heaven. Still such luxuries are unknown amongst miners and there were only three men who could wear a collar, amongst all those present, and they ran a considerable risk for it was seriously considered whether we should fine them 5 dollars each for breaking the miners etiquette. I flatter myself, Nell would have considered me as charming as ever, with my blue jersey and black tail coat. Well, at midnight we reassembled and the toast The Queen was drunk with hearty goodwill amidst the squealing of the band playing the National Anthem, the band consisting of a violin, clarionette, and guitar. Then followed songs, comic and otherwise with stump speeches, recitations, etc. and the following toasts at intervals—

Great Britain and Colonies
Navy, Army & Reserve Forces
Absent Friends at Home
Atlin District
The Ladies
Our American Cousins

These toasts provoked some good speeches and most present felt a lump in their throat whilst we drank to Absent Friends at Home. But we all sang or tried to sing a verse of Home Sweet Home, some of us shouting our loudest in order to keep something like moisture from our eyes. Well, we soon banished all unnerving thoughts and the fun ran high, song after song was called for and it was not until half past six in the morning that any one thought of retiring. At that time the party ended with Auld Lang Syne & God Save the Queen and so ended a Christmas Dinner and party that will live long in the memories of all present.

From *Writing Home to Dorset from the Yukon, 1898.*

Sending a young, sickly Englishman to the Klondike for his health seems rather drastic, but twenty-three-year-old William White was advised to work outdoors. Anxious to make enough money to marry his fiancée, Nell, he headed North. Optimistic about his chances of finding gold, he worked fruitlessly on claims in the Atlin area, finally doing odd jobs in several Yukon communities to keep himself alive. Throughout, his optimism never wavered. Later, penniless in Whitehorse, he got a job at the Canadian Bank of Commerce, but employees were not allowed to marry unless their salaries were deemed sufficient—and Will's was not. After a brief trip home to the patient Nell, he returned to the bank, working in various towns in British Columbia before resigning from the bank—where he still was not making enough money to marry—but instead he was promoted and Nell came to Canada. He retired in 1932 as the bank's Custodian of Securities in Vancouver. He was a member of the British Columbian Philatelic Society, befitting this faithful letter writer.

Yukon Yesterdays

by Major Nevill Armstrong

hristmas Eve and 255 miles from civilization. I wonder who would change places with us? After all, we are very happy and comfortable so long as good health remains with us. We have plenty to eat, glorious air, invigorating, tempered with the excitement of delving for gold. It is true our fortune hangs on the results of our prospecting work, but with this we are gambling for a big stake. I pray for everyone's sake that we may meet with success. Very busy to-day helping Marion to decorate and prepare for tomorrow. We are giving a dinner-party and our guests will be Leith and his wife, and Pom. Cut fir trees and decorated the cabin inside and out and then helped Pom decorate his cabin. Cooked supper for Marion, who was busy making things look nice in the cabin. After supper Pom and I scrubbed the floor, which was getting horribly dirty. Felt awfully tired to-night. I wonder what they are all doing at home.

Monday, December 25th, 11 degrees above

Christmas Day. Marion gave me a present of a hand-knitted silk tie, a box of her own make of sweets, the box in which the sweets were placed she had made of birch bark. She gave Pom a hand-worked case for his razors, etc., and Leith a pair of knitted woolen gloves. At 4 p.m., after having taken Marion for a sleigh-ride, we commenced cooking operation. We borrowed Pom's table and Marion made it look awfully attractive with a white table cloth, a drawn-work centre, hand made paper flowers and little baskets of sweets, also dinner-napkins. Our dinner consisted of soup (moose), ptarmigan and sausage, plum-pudding, mince pie and rum and whisky. Mrs. Leith accompanied Leith in his songs on the violin (which was rather trying!) and I played them selections on the gramophone. Old Pom got a little heady and no wonder! the rum was exceedingly strong. We drank to our dear ones near and far and thought continuously of our little daughter.

From *Yukon Yesterdays*.
   For several years Nevill Armstrong managed the Yukon Gold Fields Co. Ltd. on Russell Creek, a tributary of the Stewart River, for a group of British investors. Little gold was found.

Plum Pudding

To be made well before Christmas.
1 1/2 pounds raisins (after stoning)
1/2 pound of currants (washed and dried)
1/2 pound of mixed peel
1/4 pound of chopped almonds
3/4 pound of fresh white bread crumbs
3/4 pound of suet (minced or chopped fine)
8 eggs
1 to 2 wine glasses of brandy or white rum

Mix dry ingredients together. Beat eggs. Add to mixture. Stir well until all blended. Pack into buttered basin, tie with clean cloth and boil for 5 to 6 hours.
Can also be boiled in cloth.
Sprinkle generously with brandy or rum to preserve, wrap tightly and store in a cool place.
On Christmas day, put in boiling water and boil for 2 hours. Unmold and dust with sugar before serving. Can pour a little brandy over pudding and light at the time of serving.
Serves 6 to 8 people.

Bennett News

January 2, 1901

 he Christmas tree on Christmas Eve was a great success. Nearly everyone in Bennett was present and quite a contingent of ladies and gentlemen came over from Log Cabin.

The church was decorated with evergreens, flags and festoons of Chinese lanterns, reflecting the greatest credit on Mrs. Carmichael and Mrs. de Bellefuille, assisted by Mrs. Fowler, Mrs. Nicolson and Mrs. Booth and several gentlemen. The tree was a very large one and reached from floor to ceiling; it was heavily laden with presents for children and adults. So artistic was the whole effect that upon entering the church one seemed to be ushered into fairyland. The first part of the evening was devoted to music, when a program was rendered, and every item being loudly applauded.

Punctually at 9:30 as expected, Santa Claus arrived at the door to the intense delight of the juveniles. After exchanging greetings with those around him he proceeded to distribute his gifts to the satisfaction of everyone present and then he bid everybody good night, promising to come again next year. Much laughter was occasioned at the nature of some of the presents of which the gentlemen were recipients. Rev. Mr. Russell gave each of the Sunday School children a nicely bound story book.

From the *Whitehorse Star.*
  During the Gold Rush, Bennett was a "town" at the head of Lake Bennett and at the headwaters of the Yukon River. Having successfully negotiated the Chilkoot Pass, the stampeders arrived here to begin the descent of the Yukon River system to the Klondike. They hand-sawed lumber from the trees in the neighborhood and built a range of imaginative craft for the 400-mile journey downriver.

A Klondike Wedding, Christmas Day 1904

by Rev. George Pringle

our miles down the snow trail and across the creek valley, and I was at Last Chance Roadhouse. The wedding party was waiting for me when I arrived. The roadhouse was a low, log building about fifty feet long and twenty wide. There were no partitions. The bar was at one end, the kitchen at the other, and the part in between was a sort of "Anyman's Land." It was dining-room, parlor and gambling room in one. The bunk-house was separate. Things were "humming" from kitchen to bar, for remember it was Christmas at a roadhouse on a main creek trail in the Klondike in early days. The place was crowded with men of all sorts and all nations. Women of ill-repute were there, gambling was going on, the bar was doing a big business, the air was thick with smoke and noisy with ribald, drunken songs and laughter.

Not the most suitable place in the world for a wedding. For all that, it went through in fine style. We stood up beside the table and they all grew quiet. A blanket was hung up by the roadhouse man in front of the bar— done because of his innate sense of the fitness of things. There was no bothersome noise, except the opening and closing of the doors as people came in and went out, and the stage-whispering of a few men in the bar who were too far along with their celebrations for their fellows to control them completely.

The names of the bride and groom, their true names, were, Jensine Kolken and John Peczu Kazinsky. She was a Norwegian Lutheran, he a Hungarian Roman Catholic, married by a Canadian Presbyterian minister in a Klondike roadhouse. Rather an unusual combination but it turned out splendidly. They loved one another sincerely and all these years have lived happily. They are prosperous and have several children.

After the wedding many toasts were drunk. I drank mine in soda-water. Before the toasts Mrs. Kazinsky had gone to the kitchen and was there busy about supper. She was the roadhouse cook and had a lot of work to do that must be done without delay, preparing and serving meals to the holiday crowd. I said good-bye, put on parka and mitts, and set out on my seven mile tramp to Gold Bottom, where we had arranged a Camp Christmas Tree Entertainment for that night.

It was cold, bitter cold, the roadhouse thermometer said 50 below zero, and yet it was a grand night. We had seen no sun night or day for weeks, but for all that it was as clear as day with a light more beautiful than that of the sun. The whole broad, snow-white gulch around me was flooded with light. I looked up to the sky and there my eyes beheld a wondrous sight, magnificent beyond imagining. The dome of heaven, from east to west and from north to south, was filled with an iridescent misty glory, glowing with strange light in which gleamed lovely, delicate shades of green and gold. You could see this luminous mist and yet see through it as if it weren't there at all. It was almost uncanny, like seeing the invisible. In the midst of it floated the moon at the full, ablaze with abundant light, spilling it down in wasteful abundance mixed with the Aurora, coming to the silent earth to change it to a glistening, white fairyland of unrivalled beauty. Far, far beyond in the clear depths of the cloudless sky a thousand, thousand stars sparkled intensely like well-set jewels. As I gazed the misty glory disappeared as if by magic and in its place I saw great arrows of witching light shooting in masses back and forth through the air.

I stood, as many times I did those winter nights, spell-bound and reverent in the presence of God's handiwork. Fancy took wing. Perchance this fair light was from the shining pinions of angels as they flew hither and thither on heavenly errands. Perchance it was the gleaming from a myriad spears, as the armies of the Lord of Hosts marched and countermarched in some Grand Parade. Or were these the wild, elemental forces of nature playing at games that the Creator had taught them and that they had played from all eternity?

Apart from these dreamings, I know I shall never see anything, with my mortal eyes at least, so startlingly and mystically beautiful as these canvasses which God hangs out night after night in the far North for all to see who will but lift up their eyes to the heavens.

From *Adventures in Service*.
George Pringle first went North to Atlin, for the summer, in 1900 to fill in for his brother, Reverend John Pringle, the Presbyterian minister. In 1901 George went to the Klondike where he spent the next ten years, a friend to the miners. He was ordained in Dawson in 1902, the farthest north that an ordination had been held. He served in the First World War. Following the war, he was a prime mover in the unification of the Presbyterian, Methodist and some Baptist churches.

Northern Childhood

by Evelyn Berglund Shore

ecember was a big month for us, for Hazel's birthday was the eighteenth, George's the twenty-second, and Charley's the twenty-third. Then came Christmas. But sometimes there wasn't much we could do about it. I especially remember the Christmas of 1926, when I was nine.

On Christmas Eve the sky was cloudy and a cold wind was blowing. Outside the thermometer said twenty below zero. Mother told us to go to bed and get a good night's sleep, because tomorrow would be Christmas, and when we asked if we were going to have a tree, even though we had no presents to open, she said she thought Dad had a tree to put up, but now to go to bed.

Christmas morning came, dark and cloudy; not even a star peeped through the windows. I opened my eyes once, then closed them and cuddled down closer to my sister. What was there to get up for? It was cold and dreary and we wouldn't have anything nice or special for Christmas. I didn't even want to get up a half hour later when I heard Mother clattering the pans as she started to cook breakfast. Our cabin had only one room, but I didn't even care to open my eyes and look at her. I didn't care to see the dark shadows that the coal-oil lamp made. They scared me, reminding me of the ghost stories Dad often told us after we had turned in for the night.

I heard Mother putting dishes on the table, and then I heard her say, "George, we're ready," and heard the striking of a match.

"Get up, kids!" she called. "Breakfast's ready."

We wiggled and groaned. "Hurry," she said. "Dress fast."

Then we got up and looked around, and the cabin was filled with the red glow of candlelight and in the middle of the room stood the prettiest Christmas tree I had ever seen. The silver and gold stars, the crescents and the bells that we had been making from cardboard and from the tinfoil of tea packages and Dad's tobacco cans all through the fall were hanging on it, and gold tinsel and colored-paper chains were thrown over the branches.

Each long branch was tipped with a red, blue, green, or yellow candleholder with a little candle of another color in it. The house was lighted only by the tiny candles. Nearer the trunk of the tree were hanging little pink paper baskets. We looked: raisins. There were little packages wrapped in red or green crepe paper. Each contained a candied fig. At the foot of the tree lay six large packages, all long and looking very much alike except that each had the name of a different one of us on it.

I don't know how I got into my clothes; I do know I didn't want to eat my breakfast. When Mother told us we could open our packages we just stood and looked until she put them in our arms. "Go ahead, open them. When you're ready, there are a little pink basket and three little packages for each of you on the tree. You may take them off yourselves."

Each package contained a big rag doll. Mine had a deep purple silk dress. It was so pretty that I've forgotten the dresses the other two girl dolls had on. The boy's dolls wore little shirts and overalls. Mother had made the six dolls and dressed them at night, after we were asleep. They were of canvas, stuffed with moose hair, their faces embroidered with colored yarns, and each had yarn hair.

From *Born on Snowshoes*.
As a child, Evelyn Berglund Shore spent nine years with her family and an old trapper friend running a trap line north of the Arctic Circle.

A Gift of Sun

by E. Hazard Wells

On Friday, December 24, we broke camp at 8:50 a.m., with the thermometer indicating 20 degrees below zero. Two hours later we reached Henderson Creek and beheld rude signboards sticking up from out of the snow with inscriptions of various camps. One of these signs bore the legend "Dr. Smith, Physician." Alas, Dr. Smith was advertising! Perhaps he thought that the outside world would never hear of it. I have told on him, however, and the medical societies will doubtless turn the doctor down when he comes home for publishing his business in the Arctic snows.

Light refracted off fine ice crystals creates sun dogs, so named because they guard the low, winter sun.

We passed Henderson Creek, Stewart and White Rivers, on this date, and camped late Christmas Eve in two feet of snow, opposite three large mountains. We had a late and very uncomfortable supper and finally sank off to sleep dreaming of the holidays.

Saturday was Christmas and the weather clerk sent the mercury to 34 below zero, but swept the sky clear of clouds for the first time in many days. During the mid-winter season, the sun circling low in the horizon is generally hidden beneath the mountains, but this day, as we traveled, there came a glorious burst of sunshine at high noon gleaming over the mountain peak and flashing a warm radiance into our faces. It was the first time in five weeks that we had seen the rubicund visage of old Sol. It seemed like a Christmas gift, that sunshine. Jack Frost, standing on the summit of one of the hills to the southward, could to all appearances have jabbed an icicle into the bottom of the sun, so close was the latter to the bottom of the hill. Our Christmas Day march was fourteen miles in length, and our camp was pitched in the spruce woods at 3 p.m.

From *Magnificence and Misery*.
    E. Hazard Wells, a reporter and photographer for the Scripps-McCrae newspaper chain, had already been in Alaska twice before he was dispatched to the Klondike in 1897 to report on the Gold Rush. His eyewitness account of the gold fever that drew men northward is based on his dispatches to the *Cincinnati Post* and illustrated with his photographs.

Liard River Madness

by Charles Camsell

On December 14th, we were at old abandoned Toad River Post. The temperature was 25° below zero and there were about eight hours of daylight. Shortly before Christmas, when we were in camp near Hell's Gate, Pelly and I undertook to make a reconnaissance trip upriver about 125 miles to the point where Turnagain River joins the Liard, in order to get some idea of travel conditions on the river. We knew that there was a small trading Post at that point, known as Muddy River Post, operated by an old friend of mine by the name of Scott Simpson, a connection of the former Governor of the Hudson's Bay Company, Sir George Simpson.

We particularly wanted to find out if we were going to be able to get through the Grand Canyon of the Liard on snowshoes, because we had no knowledge that any party had ever attempted to traverse this part of the river in wintertime. We knew also that, apart from McConnell's geological party ten years earlier, practically no travellers had been through the canyon at any time of the year since the route was abandoned as a trade route by the Hudson's Bay Company more than thirty years earlier.

The Grand Canyon of the Liard—as it was named by McConnell—is forty miles in length. It had a bad reputation throughout the whole north country, and it constitutes so effective a barrier between the Indians of the lower river and those of the upper that there was never any contact or intercourse between them. Its character may be gauged by some of the names in this portion of the river; Hell's Gate at the lower entrance, the Devil's gorge and portage at the upper end, and the Rapid of the Drowned about a third of the way up, all names given by the early voyageurs and indicating the sinister nature of the stream.

The Canyon has been cut by the river into the northern extremity of the Rocky Mountains where these mountains began to dip down and die away northward into the plateau of the Nahanni River region. It is not very deep but has steep rocky walls which can only be ascended with difficulty in a few places. Through this gash the river rushes with such tremendous speed that a canoe was once reported to have descended from the Devil's portage to Hell's Gate, forty miles, in a little over two hours....

Pelly and I entered the Canyon at Hell's Gate on December 21st. We found the surface pretty smooth, but the going was rather heavy on account of the depth of snow. We found also that the canyon was generally frozen over at the Rapid of the Drowned near which we camped on our second night out. On Christmas Day we were at the upper end of the canyon. We had tried on that day to make our way through the Devil's Gorge, but found this impossible because the force of the stream had kept the water open from wall to wall of the gorge. The only alternative was the portage of four miles over a mountain spur 1,000 feet high by a trail which had never been used in winter and only once in the summer in the last thirty years. This was the notorious Devil's portage, the evil reputation of which was responsible for the abandonment of the Liard River as a trade route from the Mackenzie to the Yukon.

It was not easy to find and follow the old trail, now snow covered to a depth of three feet. Also it was badly overgrown with trees and only here and there could we find an ingrown blaze to indicate the course of the portage trail. The climb of 1,000 feet was pretty heavy going on account of the deep snow and we had to take turns in breaking the trail ahead of the dogs.

We were on the summit by the time the sun began to set and we were ready to make camp. It was the strangest Christmas I ever spent. Certainly nobody had ever spent Christmas Day on Devil's portage before and I am sure no one has done it since. Indeed, it is quite possible that no one has ever crossed Devil's portage in wintertime, either before or after our visit.

For Pelly and me, it was an unforgettable occasion because, in addition to our usual fare of bacon, beans and bannock, we had saved a tin of plum pudding which had come all the way from England and was reserved for this day. More remarkable still, however, was Pelly's contribution when he pulled out of his kit a small flask of brandy which he had carried since July without arousing suspicion from anyone. He had kept it for an emergency, and we both felt that that emergency had arisen on Christmas night on the top of Devil's portage.

Baked Beans

1 pound navy beans
pinch of salt and pepper
1 or 2 chopped onions
1/2 pound bacon

Wash beans well. Soak in cold water overnight.
Put in pot with onions and salt and cover with water.
Fry bacon, add to pot with bacon grease from pan.
Cover and cook in slow oven for 4 hours or simmer over low heat. Add water if needed.

From *Son of the North*.

Born in Fort Liard, a remote fur-trading post in the Northwest Territories in 1876, Charles Camsell grew up among prospectors, traders and native people. His strong love of the North prompted him to travel the waterways of the Yukon and Northwest Territories and explore the land. He was variously employed as a teacher, mail carrier, prospector, writer and explorer. Later he became a geologist and worked with the Geological Survey of Canada, in 1920 becoming a Deputy Minister of Mines and Resources. He closed his career in the public service as Commissioner of the Northwest Territories from 1935–46.

Strictly speaking, this is not a Klondike story. Toad River is in northern British Columbia, as is the stretch of Liard River that Camsell writes about here. It is included because it describes the routine hardships that were accepted without question, and mostly with good humor, by the men who explored northern Canada.

Klondike Party

ost Sourdoughs who spent the winter of 1897 in Dawson will remember "Ma" Huson's Christmas party.

Survivors of that colorful Klondike Stampede are fast thinning out, but those who are still around will enjoy the story of jovial "Ma" Huson who, with her just as popular husband, "Billy" Huson, who was a professional musician and leader of several orchestras up north, spent several years in the Klondike and later in Nome where Bill Huson was a member of the City Council.

Lena and Bill Huson left Everett, Wash. in the fall of 1893, for Juneau, Alaska. As they had just been married they decided on a honeymoon trip on the Steamer *Topeka*. There was a steamship rate war on between the *Topeka* and the *Willapa* and the fare was only $5 to Juneau and this fitted their financial condition admirably. The 1893 depression had developed into a real panic.

In Juneau they embarked in the hotel business and remained there until the early spring of 1897 when they decided to join the stampede to the Klondike going over the Chilcoot Pass, and packing over that summit the only piano that was ever taken over it. They arrived in Dawson right behind the outgoing ice in the Yukon in early May 1897.

The piano was the first to arrive in the Klondike metropolis and was sold almost immediately to Harry Ash for $1200. It cost Huson $125 in Juneau. It was played at the first dance held in Dawson in June 1897, the occasion being the opening of the A. C. Co.'s new warehouse just completed. At this dance, only four white women were present: Mrs. Huson, Mrs. Yeager, Mrs. Jack Horn, and Mrs. Georgia Grant, but a number of [Indian women] from Moosehide village were interested spectators.

Dawson was a lusty, hustling young mining camp that summer and fall of 1897, and of course most new arrivals were consumed with the ambition to build cabins for shelter and get established for the coming winter so they could go out and do some prospecting. The very serious threat of a shortage of provisions for the coming winter worried everyone as the old Yukon was very low that summer and steamers were having trouble getting over the Flats below Circle city.

By September the food shortage had become critical and the Mounted Police by direction of Capt. Constantine had posted notices around town notifying all that did not have sufficient grub to last them through the winter or until the following June to leave at once for Fort Yukon where provisions were plentiful. Free transportation was provided for those who did not have the necessary means.

A remarkable situation developed from the critical shortage of provisions.

Here were miners running around town with pokes full of gold and owning rich claims, offering almost any price for grub to keep them alive through the winter. Had many of them not taken the advice of the Police and gone down the river to Fort Yukon or Circle, they probably would have starved or died from scurvy and malnutrition in spite of their gold. Gold seemed to have no value. Grub was the most important asset that winter of 1897.

Soon after the river froze in late October and the sun disappeared behind the hill back of town to remain hidden until the following March, a bleak gray winter set in over the little mining camp. The people were none too jubilant over the outlook for a long spell of monotonous diet of bacon and beans. The only entertainment was provided by the saloons, gambling houses and dance halls. Even whiskey was scarce and was selling for a dollar a sluice. I call it sluice because it contained much water. Candles were scarce at a dollar each. Coal oil was a bargain if you could find it, at $25 a gallon. Flour was usually $125 for a fifty pound sack. Sugar was almost unobtainable. No restaurants because there was no grub. And no laundries.

With Christmas in the offing, "Ma" Huson decided it would help the morale of the Community to have a little Christmas party. It started humbly enough, inviting a few of her log cabin neighbors to drop in for a bit of Christmas cheer. It seemed everyone who dropped in brought with them some morsel of food or beverage that was thought unavailable. They had no turkey, chicken, no oranges, cranberries or other delicacies, but Capt. Hansen, John Raap and Charlie Debney of the Alaska Commercial Company sent over a half dozen cans of plum pudding, some canned fruit and same candles. They also sent some candy that was designed to be sold to the Indian children. There were no children in town so they decided they would send the plum pudding and the candy to the hospital.

John J. Healy of the N. A. T. and T. Co. sent over a couple of hams, some dessicated potatoes and five gallons of claret.

Among the women who joined wholeheartedly in the party were Mrs. Ralph Boyker, Mrs. Yaeger, Mrs. Laiblin, Mrs. Georgia Grant, and Flo Hamburg.

The Huson cabin was located on Second Avenue about half a block north of the Regina Hotel, and the news of the little party spread like a prairie fire and the place was soon crowded to over flowing. Mr. Boyker and Tom Kirkpatrick, whose cabins were directly behind the Husons and facing the river, opened their homes, only a few steps away, to accommodate the party.

Upon the arrival of the claret from Healy they decided to have some punch. They used canned fruit juice, citric acid and a little "hootch" that some old sourdough had brought along. The punch bowl was a prize attraction. It had been cut out of a coal oil can—the side cut out. Five gallons of punch did not last long and a man was kept busy hauling water from the river to keep them supplied. George Appel the tinner came along and soon saw the need for another punch bowl, left for his tinshop and was back in a few minutes with another punch bowl, professionally designed from another coal oil can.

Someone had brought a single lemon, presumably for a single lemonade, but the ladies decided it was too valuable to be used for the punch and that they would save it and later take it to the hospital. It would be welcome medicine for some poor scurvy patient, and there were quite a few of them at Father Judge's hospital. By mid-afternoon seemingly every one in town was beating a path to the Huson cabin and taking keen interest in the party. Even some miners who were down from Bonanza and Eldorado dropped in to help

celebrate. The miners brought liquor in original containers, which was used for the punch. Mrs. Boyker had cooked the hams in a wash boiler, and they had plenty of coffee, so they served sandwiches and coffee in Mrs. Huson's cabin and in Mrs. Boyker's cabin, with Mrs. Yaeger and Mrs. Grant assisting.

Late in the afternoon Howard Hamilton Hart, who had a lease on Carmack's discovery claim on Bonanza volunteered to take the ladies to the Hospital with his dog team. Too many ladies for one sleigh so Paul Denhart, who had a cabin close by furnished the needed transportation with his dog team. They took along the plum pudding, the candy and the lemon, and some ham sandwiches. They were warmly received by Father Judge. The hospital was overcrowded with some patients in tents nearby. There was considerable typhoid showing up in the camp and Father Judge was sorely pressed to take care of his patients. He was grateful to the ladies for their kindly gesture. He was particularly anxious that civic minded citizens should know about the crowded condition at the little hospital and blessed the ladies for their kindly interest.

The author of this unpublished manuscript from the Yukon Archives is unknown.

A Musical Evening

by Lulu Alice Craig

hristmas eve we passed at the home of friends and with them partook of a delicious lunch just before twelve, after which we all went to the Catholic Church with a mutual friend to attend Midnight Mass and hear the good singing. The soprano was a native of Belgium and sang very sweetly with a voice of culture. Christmas day we decorated our home with evergreens, vines and some ferns, that we had gathered and pressed in the fall. Upon Christmas night we entertained a number of friends and our little girl enjoyed her Christmas tree and the expressions of kind thoughts, which our friends took pleasure in making. We had some fine mandolin music, accompanied by the guitar, and our voices chimed together in making merry the Christmas in the Klondyke.

The following Saturday evening we ate five o'clock dinner with friends, a young married couple from Chicago, and that evening much the same company that composed our Christmas gathering met with these friends to watch the old year out and the new year in.

The night was quite cold but clear and a lovely moon shone forth. We passed several hours with games and music, and when twelve o'clock came, we all stepped out upon the little veranda and listened to the various whistles and sounds made by the Dawsonites to welcome the year 1899. Several of our party joined in with the bugle calls on the cornet.

Somewhat chilled, we went in and were gladdened by a dainty lunch. After wishing each the other "Many happy returns of the day," we bade our host and hostess good-night and began to descend from the eminence upon which their home stood. I think it took one hundred and ninety steps to reach the street and there was much merriment as now and then one of us would fall. So ended our holidays, and pleasant they were, even though we were deprived of home and dear ones, and were so far away from the rest of the world.

From *Glimpses of Sunshine and Shade in the Far North*.
In January 1898, Lulu Craig, a young school teacher from Missouri, took a year's leave of absence to visit the Klondike, "giving me a rest from my school labors and widening my knowledge of the North." She, her brother and his family, spent a year in Dawson. Her book describes the people, the scenery and the wild flowers she encountered.

A Klondike Christmas

by Jack London

Mouth of the Stuart River,
North West Territory,
December 25, 1897.

My dearest Mother:

Here we are, all safe and sound, and snugly settled down in winter quarters. Have received no letters yet, so you can imagine how we long to hear from home. We are in the shortest days of the year, and the sun no longer rises, even at twelve o'clock.

Uncle Hiram and Mr. Carter have gone to Dawson to record some placer claims and to get the mail, if there is any. They took the dogs and sled with them, as they had to travel on the ice. We did expect them home for Christmas dinner, but I guess George and I will have to eat alone.

I am to be cook, so you can be sure that we'll have a jolly dinner. We will begin with the staples first. There will be fried bacon, baked beans, bread raised from sourdough, and —

He seemed perplexed, and after dubiously scratching his head a couple of times, laid down the pen. Once or twice, he tried to go on, but eventually gave it up, his face assuming a very disgusted expression. He was a robust young fellow of eighteen or nineteen, and the merry twinkle which lurked in his eyes gave the lie to his counterfeited displeasure.

It was a snug little cabin in which he sat. Built of unbarked logs, measuring not more than ten by twelve feet on the inside, and heated by a roaring Yukon-stove, it seemed more homelike to him than any house he had ever lived in, except— of course, always the one, real home.

The two bunks, table and stove occupied two-thirds of the room but every inch of space was utilized. Revolvers, rifles, hunting-knives, belts and clothes hung from three of the walls in picturesque confusion; the remaining one being hidden by a set of shelves, which held all their cooking utensils. Though already eleven o'clock in the morning, a sort of twilight prevailed outside, while it would have been quite dark within, if it had not been for the slush-lamp. This was merely a shallow, tin cup, filled with bacon grease. A piece of cotton caulking served for a wick; the heat of the flame melting the grease as fast as required.

He leaned his elbows on the table and became absorbed in a deep scrutiny of the lamp. He was really not interested in it, and did not even know he was looking at it, so intent was he in trying to discover what else there could possibly be for the dinner.

The door was thrown open at this moment, and a stalwart young fellow entered with a rush of cold air, kicking off his snow shoes at the threshold.

"Bout time for dinner, isn't it?" he asked gruffly, as he took off his mittens. But his brother Clarence had just discovered that "bacon," "beans" and "bread" all began with "b," and did not reply. George's face was covered with ice, so he contented himself with holding it over the stove to thaw. The rattle of the icy chunks on the sheet-iron was getting monotonous, when Clarence deigned to reply by asking a question.

"What's 'b' stand for?"

"Bad, of course," was the prompt answer.

"Just what I thought," and he sighed with great solemnity.

"But how about the dinner? You're cook. It's time to begin. What have you been doing? Oh! Writing! Let's see."

His jaw fell when he got to "bacon, beans and bread," and he said, "It won't do to write home that that's all we've got for Christmas dinner. It would make them worry, you know. Say, haven't we some dried apples?"

"Half a cup. Not enough for a pie."

"They'll swell, you ninny. Sit down and add apple pie to that list of yours. And say dumplings, too, while you're at it. We can make a stagger at them— put two pieces of apple in two lumps of dough, and boil them. Never say die. We'll make them think we're living like princes when they read that."

Clarence did as directed, and then sat with such a look of query on his face as to make George nervous and doubtful.

"Pretty slim, after all," he mused. "Let's see if we can't find something else—bread, flapjacks and—and—why flour-gravy, of course."

"We can bake, and boil, and fry the beans," Clarence suggested, "but what's to be done with the bacon except to fry it, I can't see."

"Why parboil it; that makes another course, nine altogether. How much more do you want, anyway?" And then to change the subject, "How cold do you think it is?"

Clarence critically studied the ice which had crept far up the cracks in the door, and then gave his judgement; "Past fifty."

"The spirit thermometer gives sixty-five, and it's still falling." George could not prevent an exultant ring in his voice, though if he had been asked why, he would not have known.

"And water freezes at thirty-two above zero," Clarence began to calculate. "That makes ninety-seven degrees of frost. Phew! Wouldn't that open the eyes of the folks at home!"

So, like the two boys that they were, they temporarily forgot their monotonous fare in an exciting discussion on the whys and wherefores of cold. But when one is afflicted with a healthy appetite he can not escape from it for very long at a time, and at twelve o'clock they set about cooking their slender meal.

George went into the cache for bacon, and began to rummage about in odd places to see what he could find. Now the cache, or place where their food was stored to keep it away from the perpetually hungry native dogs, was built onto the back of the cabin. Clarence heard the racket he was making and when he began to cheer and cry out "Eureka! Eureka!" he ran out to see what had happened.

"Manna! brother mine! Manna! dropped from the clouds for the starving children of Israel!" he cried, waving a large can above his head. "Mock-turtle soup. Found it in the tool box," he went on, as they carried it into the cabin.

True enough; it was a quart-can of specially prepared and very rich mock-turtle soup. They sang and danced and were as jubilant as though they had found a gold mine. Clarence added the item to the bill of fare in his letter, while George strove to divide it up into two items, or even more. He showed a special aptitude for this kind of work; but how many tempting dishes he would have finally succeeded in evolving out of it shall never be known, for at that moment they heard a dog team pull up the river bank before the cabin.

The next instant the door opened, and two strangers came in. They were grotesque sights. Their heads were huge balls of ice, with little holes where their mouths should have been, through which they breathed. Unable to open their mouths or speak, they shook hands with the boys and headed for the stove. Clarence and George exchanged glances and watched their strange visitors curiously.

"Wal, it's jes' this way," one of them began, as he shook the remaining chunks of ice from his whiskers, "me an' my pard ha' ben nigh on two months, now, over on the Mazy May, with nothin' to eat but straight meat. Nary flour, nary beans, nary bacon. So me an' him sorto' talked it over, an' figgered it out. At last I sez, 'Wot yeh say, Jim? Let's cross the divide an' strike some camp on the Yukon, an' git some civilized grub again? Git a reg'lar Christmas dinner?' An he sez, 'I'll go yeh, by gum.' An' here we be. How air yeh off fer meat? Got a hunderd pound or so, on the sled outside."

Just as Clarence and George were assuring him that he was heartily welcome, the other man tore away the last hindrance to his speech, and broke in; "Say, lads; yeh haint got a leetle bit o' bread yeh might spare. I'm that hungry fer jes' a leetle bit—"

"Yeh jes' shet up, Jim!" cried his partner indignantly. "Ye'd make these kids think yeh might be starvin'. Haint yeh had all yeh wanted to eat?"

"Yes," was the gloomy reply; "but nothin' but straight meat."

However, Clarence put an end to the discussion by setting the table with sour-dough bread and cold bacon, having first made them promise not to spoil their appetites for the dinner. The poor fellows handled the heavy bread reverently, and went into ecstasies of delight over it. Then they went out, unharnessed the dogs, and brought some magnificent pieces of moose meat in with them. The boys' mouths watered at the sight, for they were longing for it just as much as the others longed for the bread.

"Porterhouse moose-steak," whispered George; "tenderloin, sirloin, and round; liver and bacon; rib-roast of moose, moose stew and fried sweet breads. Hurry, Clarence, and add them to the bill of fare."

"Now don't bother me. I'm cook, and I'm going to boss this dinner, so you obey orders. Take a piece of that meat and go down to the cabin on the next island. They'd give most anything for it, so see that you make a good trade."

The hungry strangers sat on the bunk and watched proceedings with satisfied countenances, while Clarence mixed and kneaded the dough for the baking of bread. In a short time George returned, with one cup of dried apples and five of prunes. Yet they were all disappointed at his failure to get sugar. But the dinner already promised to be such a grand affair that they could readily forego such a trifling matter as sweets.

Just as Clarence was shortening the pie-dough with bacon grease, a second sled pulled up at the door, and another stranger entered. A vivid picture he made, as he stood for an instant in the doorway. Though his eyebrows and lashes were matted with ice, his face was clean-shaven, and hence, free from it. From his beaded moccasins to his great gauntleted mittens and wolf-skin cap from Siberia, every article of wearing apparel proclaimed him to be one of the "Eldorado Kings," or millionaire mine-owners of Dawson.

He was a pleasant man to look at, though his heavy jaw and steel-blue eyes gave notice of a firm, indomitable will. About his waist was clasped a leather belt, in which reposed two large Colt's revolvers and a hunting-knife, while in his hand, besides the usual dog whip, he carried a smokeless rifle of the largest bore and latest pattern. They wondered at this, for men in the Klondike rarely go armed, and then because of necessity.

His story was soon told. His own team of seven dogs, the finest in the country and for which he had recently refused five thousand dollars, had been stolen five days before. He had found the clue, and discovered that the thieves had started out of the country on the ice. He had borrowed a team of dogs from a friend and taken their trail.

They marveled at his speed, for he had left Dawson at midnight, having traveled the seventy-five miles in twelve hours. He wished to rest the animals and take a few hours sleep, before going on with the chase. He was sure of overtaking them, he said, for they had foolishly started with an eighteen-inch sled, while the regular, trail Yukon-sleds were only sixteen inches wide. Thus, they had to break trail constantly for one of the runners, while his was already broken.

They recognized the party he was after, and assured him that he was certain to catch them in another twelve hours' run. Then he was made welcome and invited to dinner. To their surprise, when he returned from unhitching and feeding his dogs he brought several pounds of sugar and two cans of condensed milk.

"Thought you fellows, up river here, would be out of luxuries," he said as he threw them upon the table; "and as I wanted to travel light, I brought them along, intending to trade for beans and flour whenever I got a chance. No, never mind thanks. I'm going to eat dinner with you. Call me when it's ready." And he climbed into one of the bunks, falling asleep a moment later.

"I say, Jim. That's travelin', aint it?" said the Man from Mazy May, with as much pride as though he had done it himself. "Seventy-five mile in twelve hours, an' thet cold he wa'nt able to ride more'n half the time. Bet ye'd be petered clean out if yeh done the like o' thet."

"Maybe yeh think I can't travel," his partner replied. But before he could tell what a wonderful traveler he was, their dogs and the dogs of the new arrival started a fight, and had to be separated.

At last the dinner was ready, and just as they were calling the "Eldorado King," Uncle Hiram and Mr. Carter arrived.

"Not an ounce of sugar or can of milk to be bought in Dawson," he said. But his jaw dropped as he caught sight of the sugar and milk on the table, and he sheepishly held up a quart-can of strained honey as his contribution.

This addition necessitated a change in the bill of fare; so when they finally sat down, the first course of mock-turtle soup was followed by hot cakes and honey. While one after another the delicacies of "civilized grub," as they called it, appeared, the eyes of the Men from Mazy May opened wider and wider, and speech seemed to fail them.

But one more surprise was in store for them. They heard a jingle of bells, and another ice-covered traveler entered and claimed their hospitality. The new-comer was an Associated Press reporter, on his way to Dawson from the United States. His first question was concerning the where-abouts of a Mr. Hiram Donaldson, "said to be camped on the Yukon near the mouth of the Stuart River." On Uncle Hiram being pointed out to him, the reporter handed him a letter of introduction from the Mining Syndicate which he, Mr. Donaldson, was representing. Nor was this all. A fat package of letters was also passed over—the long-looked-for letters from home.

"By gum! This do beat all," said the Man from Mazy May, after a place had been made for the last arrival. But his partner had his mouth so full of apple dumpling that he could only roll his eyes in approval.

"I know what 'b' stands for," whispered George across the table to Clarence.

"So do I. It stands for 'Bully' with a big 'B'."

From *Collected Short Stories of Jack London.*
Jack London was only twenty-one when he arrived in the Yukon in 1897 from California. He stayed in the Klondike less than a year, but became famous for his stories of the North. His log cabin in Dawson continues to be a tourist attraction. A prolific writer, he died at age forty.

Christmas in Old Crow

by Claude and Mary Ryder Tidd

hristmas was almost upon us before we realized it. This is unquestionably the most colourful time of the whole year amongst the natives, and a period of a great deal of merry-making. As early as mid-December, with typical native disregard of such problems as catching fur, the men and likely enough some of the women too from their remote traplines will arrive at the post. On a quiet very cold day the cheery jingling of dog-bells may be heard long before there is any sign of an approaching team. An excited voice, more than likely a childish voice will shout "Dog-team" and within two minutes everyone in camp is out of doors and there is much handshaking and welcoming the travellers. Within a week practically everyone was in post, and from now until Christmas I found my hands more than comfortably full, buying fur and generally attending to their wants.

Perhaps one of the most serious considerations is the question of the meat supply. There is of course no butcher's shop: every man is both his own hunter and butcher and the meat is either caribou or moose which has to be hunted, cut up and hauled in to camp by dog-team. The choicest joints are cut up and saved for the Christmas feasts: the question of refrigeration presents no difficulties in these latitudes at this time of the year.

There is an atmosphere of much excitement everywhere, particularly in the store. A few days before Christmas my wife and I with the willing help of some of the younger women, dressed up the shelves and show-cases with festoons of brilliantly-coloured papers, candles of every imaginable hue, sparkling tinsel ornaments and other appropriate dressings, all drawn, I strongly suspected, from our own private supply. The girls entered into all this business with unbounded enthusiasm and much childish eagerness to the accompaniment of many "O-o-ohs" and "A-a-ahs" and "We never see that kind before." And I am quite sure that it was all new to some of the smaller children, judging from their wide-eyed looks of bewildered astonishment. Unexpected catches of fur came to light in exchange for which extra supplies of tea, coffee, sugar and evaporated milk, with some luxuries such as canned peaches, canned apricots or other fruits were purchased in readiness for the expected feasts to come later. The women were thrilled with the inevitable coloured silk handkerchiefs for use as head coverings; the brighter the colours the more they were in demand. Also for the women there were bright woollen sweaters, stockings and gayly coloured dress materials. For the men there were fancy socks, ties, handkerchiefs, plenty of pipes, and—yes, believe it or not— plenty of cigarettes, though I admit that these latter were not all bought by the men.

And so our first Christmas Day at Old Crow finally dawned clear and bright with the thermometer down to thirty below zero. By eleven o'clock the church bell had called every available person in the village and the little log church was crowded, the men all grouped on one side of the aisle, the women on the other. The grown-ups in their best Sunday suits and new dresses; the bright scarves and handkerchiefs; the fancy beaded moccasins and mittens; many of the women with their babies on their backs; and the children with their caribou-skin parkas all made a never-to-be-forgotten sight in that little northern log church. As I was the only one able to do it, I had volunteered to play the tiny organ for the service. And HOW they all sang! What harmony was lacking was more than compensated for by the earnestness and enthusiasm with which everyone entered into the singing. They all enjoyed it so much, and there was no-one there to criticize. With much vigour we all sang "Oh Come All Ye Faithful" and many other of the old tunes with which most of us are familiar. But I think that the picture that will remain in my memory for a long time is the one of that row of small children standing wide-eyed in front of the organ singing "Jesus Loves Me."

From *Life in the Yukon*.
    As a young Englishman, Claude Tidd adventured to Canada and tried his hand at many jobs before heading north as a member of the North-West Mounted Police. A keen naturalist and photographer, he travelled widely in the Yukon, mostly by riverboat and dog team, and kept a careful record of his travels. He met and married an American missionary nurse, Mary Ryder, in Fort Yukon, Alaska. The Tidds ran a fur-trading post in Old Crow, some sixty miles north of the Arctic Circle. They retired to England, where Claude died shortly after. Mary returned to Lancaster, Pennsylvania where she died a few years later.

Stuffed Moose Heart

Spread heart open, and fill with stuffing.
Cover and roast in low oven.
Uncover towards the end of cooking to brown it.

Sage Dressing

Break up stale bread or bannock into medium-sized pieces.
Put in sage until the bread is green with sage dust.
Mix with one or more large onions, chopped.
Add seasonings and salt and pepper to taste.
Sprinkle with water until stuffing is moist.
If dry bread is used, soak it briefly in water before using it.

Starry Night

by Gordon Stables

erhaps the glorious aurora borealis never shone and scintillated more beautifully above the wild hills and snow-laden woods of Klondyke, than it did on that still, starry night of December 25th, 189–.

As white as the sunlight at one moment, in quivering, snake-like ribbons and fringe, so close, apparently, that you might cast a salmon fly over it, as one does over the Dee, and the next moment flickering here and there in a flush of pale crimson, sea-green, or blue.

Not a sound was to be heard over all this strange land, save now and then the wail of a wolf, or sharp, ringing bark of a fox in the distance. Except for this, it was a silence that seemed preternatural, a silence that could be felt, and gazing skywards, although one might be mistaken, it was impossible not to believe that the aurora did emit sound, partly hissing, partly crackling.

From *Off to Klondyke or A Cowboy's Rush to the Gold Fields*.
An excerpt from a fictional story written for the Boy's Adventure Library.

Sixty and Seventy Below

by Anna DeGraf

The first winter I was in Dawson I became acquainted with a widow who kept a little store. She was refined and agreeable and we soon became good friends. She was engaged to an engineer and they were to be married in the spring. She brought him to see me and he told us he had some friends who were reading together, studying theosophy, and said he would like to bring them to see us. One was a librarian, another a miner, and the third was manager of the Standard Oil Company there. They were all educated, interesting men. They came the next Sunday evening, and we continued to have these little Sunday evening meetings during the winter. One week we met at the widow's house, and the next at my cabin. The men would read a while, then a discussion followed, and afterward we had a cup of tea and some cake or other light refreshment, and at ten o'clock they all went home. Those evenings were delightful.

As Christmas drew near I suggested to the widow that we ought to do something to keep these men from getting homesick—not anything expensive, but just in a nice way, and she agreed. The librarian and the miner lived in a cabin a short distance out of town on the bank of the Klondike River, and the other men had expected to go out there on Christmas Eve. We had to take the miner into our confidence, so we could get into the cabin, and he got the Christmas tree for us.

The afternoon of December 24th the widow and I closed our stores early and the miner came for us with a sled. We had gotten together some little gifts, and toys such as one would buy for small boys—a drum, a watch, a little horn, and so on; and I took along a pair of clean curtains and put them up in place of the ones that had done service for many months. We put strings across the room near the ceiling and hung greens and toys on them; set up the Christmas tree, trimmed and lighted it, had a fire going and supper on the way, when we heard the other men coming.

We hid behind the door and waited. One of them said, "Why, Collard (the miner) must have come home early, the fire is going." On opening the door, they exclaimed "Oh, what a transformation! My land! this is wonderful!"…Then the widow tittered and they discovered us. We danced around and laughed from sheer delight. The miner lay on the floor, kicking his heels together, and tooting on a little horn, as his way of showing his joy. We put big aprons on the men and they finished getting supper, while we set the table."

Afterward we sang hymns and all the other songs we could think of. One of the men read from Shakespeare, and the others took their turns at "speaking pieces." We danced, and as we had no musical instrument except the little tin horn, we danced to our own singing. Either the singing was good or we made a lot of noise that attracted the men from the neighboring cabins

A dog team pulls a freighter sled over the river ice.

and tents, and on looking out we discovered quite a crowd, and they joined in the singing.

When one o'clock came, the men took the widow and me home on the sled—a wonderful ride in the bright, clear moonlight, although the weather was very cold. They had us promise to come again on New Year's Eve, and we went and had another happy time. A sled in that country does not mean the little ones the children have in the States, but it is a large, long, slender Yukon sled, drawn by prancing malamutes or huskies, or sometimes by men.

The people who live in large cities and are surfeited during the Holidays with a round of gaiety, who receive and give loads of handsome presents, wear beautiful clothes and eat all sorts of delicacies, haven't the faintest idea of the wholesome pleasure we had on those two occasions, and at other times, in a simple way.

From *Pioneering on the Yukon, 1892–1917*.

Concerned about the disappearance of her twenty-three-year-old prospector son, Anna DeGraf went north in 1892 to look for him. She took along her sewing machine to earn her keep. Troubled by a broken leg that had healed poorly, the fifty-three-year-old crossed the Chilkoot Pass with her crutch and made her way to Dawson. For more than twenty years she worked in Dawson as a seamstress. She never found her son. After her return to California and at age eighty-five, she wrote her memoirs; its manuscript was discovered in a trunk after her death in 1930.

Christmas Highly Enjoyed By All

Dawson, Sunday, December 27, 1903

he merry yuletide has yuled in Dawson this year as yulingly as she ever yuled before in the history of the country. Everybody had a merry Christmas. At least, those who did not have failed to report.

Beginning Thursday afternoon, Christmas continued until early yesterday, when, in the language of George Ade, more than one man in Dawson very confidently felt as though he could consume one or two barrels of water. (Boys, you know how it is.)

Thursday afternoon a raid was made on the Christmas tree at St. Mary's school and never did a tree yield more abundantly or richly. Every child was laden with toys and costly presents, fully $300 worth being distributed among the pupils. An excellent program preceded the distribution of presents, which was followed by appropriate addresses from Father Runoz and Colonel McGregor.

Thursday night there were Christmas trees at the Methodist and Presbyterian churches, excellent programs being given by the Sunday school children in both.

At St. Mary's church midnight mass was appropriately celebrated after excellent music and impressive services.

On Christmas day the Salvation Army fed the homeless and hungry, serving a meal that would do justice to Delmonico in his halcyon days.

Christmas night came the annual big dinner at the police barracks, and in the evening the town station boys were not behind their fellows at the barracks.

Private dinner parties were given in hundreds of homes, where friends met and enjoyed the occasion. At night several little parties were held and not until well along in the small hours of yesterday morning were sleeping apartments invaded. The result was that when the water man came yesterday forenoon nobody was up.

As a whole, Christmas 1903, was a howling success in Dawson, regardless of the fact that a large portion of our country is tied up in concessions.

Beaver Tail and Beans

Blister tail over a hot fire until skin loosens. Pull skin off.
Boil big pot of beans; add beaver tail. Add onion and salt. Cover and bury in hot ashes in pit for a few hours.

From *The Yukon Sun.*
The Yukon Sun was first published in Dawson in 1898; it folded in 1904.

Turkey Shoot at Carcross

December 27, 1901

r. W.A. Anderson, the Caribou hotel man, gave a turkey shooting match on Christmas in which 18 birds were put up to be contested for. Caribou can boast of more crack shots than any other town of its size in Canada, and the entire population turned out to take part in and witness the contest. A regular target was used, which was placed at a distance of 100 yards.

Everything went off smoothly. The day was fine and the sport was thoroughly enjoyed by everyone present. A noticeable feature was the entire absence of drunkenness, not an intoxicated person was present.

The Indians took an active part in the proceedings and every turkey was hotly contested for. Paddie, of Tagish, carried off the honors of the day.

Among the prize winners were: "Shorty" Austin and Tom Dixon, late of the N.W.M.P.; Hugh Tarton, Vickhardt, Skookum Jim, Tagish Paddie, Anderson, Scott, Stewart and others.

From *The Daily Evening Star*.

Carcross, a stopping point on the stampeders' route to the Klondike, was originally called Caribou Crossing. The Montana Mountain herd of caribou crossed the narrows between Tagish Lake and Lake Bennett on their annual migrations. Skookum Jim was George Carmack's partner, and a co-discoverer of the 1896 gold strike on Bonanza Creek.

The Cremation of Sam McGee

by Robert Service

There are strange things done in the midnight sun
By the men who moil for gold;
The Arctic trails have their secret tales
That would make your blood run cold;
The Northern Lights have seen queer sights,
But the queerest they ever did see
Was that night on the marge of Lake Lebarge
I cremated Sam McGee.

Now Sam McGee was from Tennessee, where the cotton blooms
    and blows,
Why he left his home in the South to roam 'round the Pole, God
    only knows.
He was always cold, but the land of gold seemed to hold him like a spell;
Though he'd often say in his homely way that "he'd sooner live in hell."

On a Christmas Day we were mushing our way over the Dawson trail.
Talk of your cold! through the parka's fold it stabbed like a driven nail.
If our eyes we'd close, then the lashes froze till sometimes we
    couldn't see;
It wasn't much fun, but the only one to whimper was Sam McGee.

And that very night, as we lay packed tight in our robes beneath
    the snow,
And the dogs were fed, and the stars o'erhead were dancing heel and toe,
He turned to me, and "Cap," says he, "I'll cash in this trip, I guess;
And if I do, I'm asking that you won't refuse my last request."

Well, he seemed so low that I couldn't say no; then he says with a sort
    of moan:
"It's the cursèd cold, and it's got right hold till I'm chilled clean through to
    the bone.
Yet 'tain't being dead—it's my awful dread of the icy grave that pains;
So I want you to swear that, foul or fair, you'll cremate my last remains."

A pal's last need is a thing to heed, so I swore I would not fail;
And we started on at the streak of dawn; but God! he looked ghastly pale.
He crouched on the sleigh, and he raved all day of his home in Tennessee;
And before nightfall a corpse was all that was left of Sam McGee.

There wasn't a breath in that land of death, and I hurried, horror-driven,
With a corpse half hid that I couldn't get rid, because of a promise given;
It was lashed to the sleigh, and it seemed to say: "You may tax your brawn
    and brains,
But you promised true, and it's up to you to cremate those last remains."

Malemutes were the dogs of choice for dog teams, but almost any animal—even goats!—
was harnessed.

Now a promise made is a debt unpaid, and the trail has its own stern code.
In the days to come, though my lips were dumb, in my heart how I cursed
    that load.
In the long, long night, by the lone firelight, while the huskies, round in
    a ring,
Howled out their woes to the homeless snows—O God! how I loathed
    the thing.

And every day that quiet clay seemed to heavy and heavier grow;
And on I went, though the dogs were spent and the grub was getting low;
The trail was bad, and I felt half mad, but I swore I would not give in;
And I'd often sing to the hateful thing, and it hearkened with a grin.

Till I came to the marge of Lake Lebarge, and a derelict there lay;
It was jammed in the ice, but I saw in a trice it was called the "Alice May."
And I looked at it, and I thought a bit, and I looked at my frozen chum;
Then "Here," said I, with a sudden cry, "is my cre-ma-tor-eum."

Some planks I tore from the cabin floor, and I lit the boiler fire;
Some coal I found that was lying around, and I heaped the fuel higher;
The flames just soared, and the furnace roared—such a blaze you
    seldom see;
And I burrowed a hole in the glowing coal, and I stuffed in Sam McGee.

Then I made a hike, for I didn't like to hear him sizzle so;
And the heavens scowled, and the huskies howled, and the wind began
    to blow.
It was icy cold, but the hot sweat rolled down my cheeks, and I don't
    know why;
And the greasy smoke in an inky cloak went streaking down the sky.

I do not know how long in the snow I wrestled with grisly fear;
But the stars came out and they danced about ere again I ventured near;
I was sick with dread, but I bravely said: "I'll just take a peep inside.
I guess he's cooked, and it's time I looked"; . . . and then the door I
    opened wide.

And there sat Sam, looking cool and calm, in the heart of the furnace roar;
And he wore a smile you could see a mile, and he said: "Please close
    that door.
It's fine in here, but I greatly fear you'll let in the cold and storm—
Since I left Plumtree, down in Tennessee, it's the first time I've been warm."

    There are strange things done in the midnight sun
    By the men who moil for gold;
    The Arctic trails have their secret tales
    That would make your blood run cold;
    The Northern Lights have seen queer sights,
    But the queerest they ever did see
    Was that night on the marge of Lake Lebarge
    I cremated Sam McGee.

From *The Collected Poems of Robert Service*.
  "The Cremation of Sam McGee" is one of Robert Service's best-loved poems, although it may have been written before the poet ever saw the Klondike. Service had wandered around the world, supporting himself by a diversity of odd jobs—gardener, dishwasher, and fruit picker, among others—before he reached the Yukon in 1904. Sam McGee reportedly was a customer at the Bank of Commerce in Whitehorse, where Service worked as a bank clerk, and the *Alice May* might have been inspired by the derelict *Olive May*, which lay in Lake LeBarge.

Sourdough Story

by Rev. George Pringle

In nearly eleven years of continuous travelling as a missionary to outlying groups on the Yukon trails, living on the creeks among the mountains in those early Klondike Gold Stampede days, I could not fail to have my share of memorable experiences, some of them with more than a spice of hazard. I lived just the regular life of a "musher"—a man on the trail—and while that mode of life assuredly held nothing of monotony, yet I grew so accustomed to it that it all seemed part of the usual, familiar, course of things.

After the summer, beautiful but brief, there came the eight months of grim, relentless winter. Then we had to face the long darkness and the deadly cold. As missionary on these outlying creeks I often travelled through vast white valleys, filled with a weird silence broken only by the howling of the wolves; and battled through deep and drifting snow along miles of lonely summits. But against each problem or task that Nature set us, we sourdoughs matched with zest our wits and skill. There was the joy and conflict of it. Experience made us self-reliant and we learned to love the life, so free and clean, so full of stirring incident and victorious combat with the elements. Only now I am commencing to get the true perspective of those colourful and happy Yukon days, when I was young and the world was young;

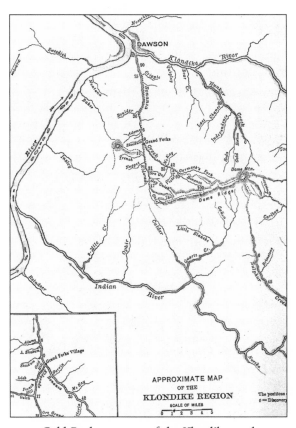

Gold Rush–era map of the Klondike creeks.

commencing to recognize how wonderfully unique and intensely interesting they were. They can never be repeated.

The Christmas festivities on the Klondike creeks long ago usually continued for about a month. The weather was so frosty that work on the windlass was both disagreeable and risky, so it became customary for the four and five mid-winter weeks to be mostly occupied in visiting or entertaining neighbours and friends. Small "parties" were held in a sort of rotation at the larger cabins up and down the valleys. Everybody was merrymaking. Hospitality knew no artificial bonds, for in the Yukon in those golden days, there was neither prince nor peasant, rich or poor. Don't think from this that we had no right social standards. I know that much of the fiction about the North is built on the theory that the men in the Klondike diggings were "rough, tough and hard to handle," with low moral codes. That assumption may make a novel "spicy" and increase its sale, but nevertheless it is quite untrue, in regard to 99 per cent of us Sourdoughs. Of course we had some of the other sort too. We had worthy moral standards, simple but definite. Our social grading was not based on the size and contents of a man's "poke"— (you would say "purse") nor on his grandfather's record. If he lived an honest decent life among us, he was barred from nothing.

In addition to the many smaller affairs, each gulch, when there were miners, would have one big evening for all, log-church or roadhouse being requisitioned for the occasion. These were called Christmas Tree Entertainments, or simply "Trees" for short, and I was usually expected to be chairman at the "Trees" at Last Chance, Gold Bottom, Gold Run, Granville and Sulphur Creek. To meet these last requirements each of my creeks had to choose a different date so that I could make the rounds.

In the winter of 1904 we had carried through our entertainments at Last Chance, Gold Bottom, Granville and Gold Run. Sulphur Creek was the last and they had been working to make it the best of all. It was to be held on December 28th.

Well, friends, here is my brief little Sourdough story of nearly forty years. I'll have to leave out a lot of details and explanations that you'll have to take for granted.

At noon, December 28th, a very happy party of six "tillicums" were gathered in Jordan's cabin on Gold Run. We were all young men then, many years ago. Jordan and his partner, Jim Prophet, were there, Coldrick and

Londoner, McGregor the Australian, Bousfield and myself. Prophet had been lucky enough to get a moose that had strayed into the valley within rifle-shot, and it lay partly cut up on some poles by the "cache." So he invited his friends in to help eat some of the choicest parts, moose-steak in ordinary being, of course, too common for a special feast. I shall forbear entering into details of that meal, but our meat dish was young moose-heart stuffed and roasted, with fresh Klondike river grayling as an entree.

We were sitting at the table when there came a knock on the door, and in response to Jordan's hearty "Come in," it was opened and the form of our good friend, Corp. Haddock of the North West Mounted Police, emerged through the mist. He sat down a minute or two, but wouldn't stay. He was calling at all the cabins giving advice that no one should attempt to leave the valley until the weather moderated. The barracks' thermometer registered 65 degrees below zero, and a very dense fog had formed. Under these conditions it was perilous to attempt any journey far away from their cabins. No one spoke of my intended trip until Haddock had gone, when Coldrick said, "That puts the finish on your mush to Sulphur, Pringle." "No," I replied, "I gave my word I'd be there and they will be looking for me. I have crossed that divide fifty times. I know every flake of snow on it."

This sounds boastful and foolhardy, but in fact it was neither. I realized what I was facing. I had fifteen miles in all to go, and only ten or twelve miles of it difficult travelling through deep snow on low sections of the summit. True, it was extremely cold, but I was suitably clothed and knew how to take care of myself, surely, after four years constantly on the trail. It wasn't two o'clock yet and I had a full six hours to travel fifteen miles. I decided to go.

I set out and made fast time until I struck the drifts on the summit. The short spell of gloom we called day had ended, and it was rapidly growing dark. Before I had gone a mile there would be no light, pitch-dark, and this unpleasant dense fog would be blindfolding my eyes as well. With it all I didn't worry. This was a difficult job that faced me, but I was in my own workshop, had my own tools, and was working at my own trade. Fate, however, had decreed that I should watch things this time.

Somehow, unwittingly, I had gradually turned a quarter circle to the right in the drifts, and was then, without knowing it, travelling *along* the low, undulating divide instead of *across* it. Laboriously but confidently I kept on through the darkness and the fog, unconscious of my error, until, after three

hours, I found myself at the foot of a grade that I had thought was the slope down into the Sulphur valley. I soon found my mistake. It must have been some immense cup-shaped depression on the divide, its bottom strewn with a fearsome tangle of fallen trees carried down by a snow or landslide. For two or three testing hours I fought my way through that piled-up brush and deep snow. When I got clear I felt myself on an up-grade.

It was a long, laborious climb out of that hateful valley and I knew now that I had lost my bearings. I had to give up all hope of reaching Sulphur in time for the Tree and was growing a trifle anxious. It was terribly cold and dark. I had been working extremely hard for hours and I was getting very hungry. I didn't care to stand still or rest. My moccasin thong had come undone and I had to take off my mitts to fix it. So sharp was the frost that in a moment or two my fingers grew too stiff to do the work and I nearly failed to tie the lace. My hands were white and numb with cold when I thrust them into my fur gauntlets, beating them against my chest as I went on. My whole body sensed the chill and threat of that momentary stop. It told me that if I were forced to take my last chance for life and try to build a fire, I would almost surely fail; to find dry wood, to prepare it, to light it, and wait nursing it into a flame sufficient to warm me would be a succession of almost hopeless chances in such deadly cold, too desperate a risk to take now unless there were no other way.

My long, wearisome climb brought me at last out above the frost-bog, and I could see the stars and from them got my bearing again. Far away to the right and left in the darkness I now knew the valleys of Gold Run and Sulphur lay, but between me and them stretched impossible miles of rough country. Puzzled a moment my eyes caught the flicker of a tiny light, low down in the north, hardly to be distinguished from the stars on the sky-line. This was indeed my "star of hope." It meant warmth, and warmth was life to me. I fixed its location and with new heart headed for it.

For six hours I travelled straight away through the brush and deep snow often up to my waist. I was soon becoming extremely exhausted and weak and felt the clutching of the icy fingers of the cold getting through my clothes, and I knew there was no time to waste. Hunger and ninety-five degrees of frost on the trail, with darkness as their ally, will soon club you into unconsciousness.

However, the game isn't lost, or won, until the referee blows the final whistle. I was determined to fight it out to the finish. The flickering light was my goal and I forgot all else. I must get to it even though I might have to crawl at last on frozen hands and feet. In the hollows I lost sight of it, picking it up again on higher ground, until after long tiring miles of exhausting mushing, when I knew I hadn't much strength left, it glimmered clear, down hill, not five hundred yards away! I'll tell you I don't think the lights in Paradise will look any more beautiful to me than did the Jo-Jo Roadhouse bonfire that night, a roadhouse on the main-ridge trail at the head of the creeks. They had a big fire outside under an iron tank melting snow for water, and it was the flame of this I had seen.

My fumbling at the door latch roused the owner from his sleep. He opened the door and pulled me stumbling in and I was safe. I had been beaten in my endeavor to get to Sulphur in time for their Tree gathering, but I was a victor in a more serious contest. I had won a game against heavy odds in which the stakes were life, or death, or maiming.

My roadhouse friend was indeed a good Samaritan to me. He gave me a greatly needed hot meal, and then tucked me into a cozy bunk where I slept like a log until noon next day. He wouldn't take any pay for it at all. He started me off early in the afternoon, well fed and rested, down a well-marked comparatively easy trail to Sulphur Creek, which I reached safely.

Sourdough Starter

Mix a thin batter of flour and water. Add a little potato water, rice water or macaroni water and a pinch of sugar.

Put mixture in a crock, cover, and hang over the stove, keeping it warm for 24 hours.

Sourdough may be used to raise bread, pancakes and doughnuts. For pancakes, use a pinch of soda.

Sourdough: Pioneers of '98 or before who have spent a winter on the Yukon.

Cheechakos: Indian word for newcomer or do-nothing.

From *The Western Recorder* magazine.

The Reverend George Pringle, who had a log church on Gold Bottom Creek, was a tireless supporter of the Klondike miners. Whatever the temperature or circumstance, no creek or cabin was too remote to visit. "Nothing was too much trouble for him, and the men loved him," recalled Mrs. Lucille Hooker, who grew up in Dawson during the Gold Rush.

Christmas Along the Trail

Tantalus, December 26, 1905

 ny person in town, who has an idea that the people out on the trail do not enjoy Christmas would have been greatly surprised if he or she could have looked in at Carmack's roadhouse, Tantalus, on the evening of Christmas day and seen the twenty happy guests of Mr. and Mrs. Rowlinson seated at a long table with turkeys and every other luxury obtainable in front of them.

After dinner the guests, among whom were miners from the Five Fingers and Tantalus coal mine, woodchoppers from the neighborhood and the police, were entertained to an impromptu concert, and the talent shown would have made the famous Welsh Glee singers take second place. About midnight the party broke up with a hearty vote of thanks to the host and hostess, everybody declaring it to have been as happy a Christmas as he or she ever spent.

From *The Whitehorse Weekly Star*, January 4, 1906.
Soon after the first flush of stampeders a winter trail carried travellers by horse-drawn sleigh between Whitehorse and Dawson. Carmack's roadhouse at Tantalus was a staging post on this trail. It is at the present settlement of Carmacks, about one hundred miles north of Whitehorse.

December

by Howard V. Sutherland

Beneath a shroud of unpolluted white,
The frozen hills lie silent and asleep;
And moveless spruce and ghostly birches keep
Their silent vigils through the endless night.

The frozen creeks, long voiceless, party veiled
'Neath drifting snow, dream fondly of the trees;
Within the woods no bird's song and no breeze
Make wondrous music when the skies have paled.

The kingly sun ne'er sends his laughing rays
To wake the hills and warm the trees and streams;
His face is hid, and hid are now the beams
That woke the world on long-dead summer days.

The patient moon with all her silent train
Of maiden stars patrols the roads on high,
And watches well all things that sleeping lie
Till Spring's first song shall waken them again.

The white world sleeps, and all is very still,
Except when rises on the frosted air
From out its chilly and forbidding lair
A lone wolf's howl, long-drawn and terrible.

From *Out of the North*.
   Nothing is known of the author of this
slim volume of poetry, published in 1913.

Permissions

Every effort has been taken to trace the ownership of copyright material used in the text. The author and publisher welcome any information enabling them to rectify any reference or credit in subsequent editions.

"Greeting," p. 5, courtesy of University of Washington Libraries (UW 2791), Seattle, WA.

"Dinner on Miller Creek," p. 6, courtesy of OMI Archives, Vancouver, B.C.

"Mrs. Bompas's Tree," p. 10, courtesy of Yukon Diocesan Board, Women's Auxiliary of the Anglican Church of Canada.

"Celebrations at Fort Reliance 1882," p. 18, courtesy of *Whitehorse Star,* Whitehorse, Y.T.

"Christmas at Moosehide," p. 23, courtesy of Gerald Isaac, Whitehorse, Y.T.

"The First Klondike Baby," p. 25, courtesy of Mrs. Edith Auckland.

"Norwegian Miners," p. 37, courtesy of the Norwegian-American Historical Association, St. Olaf College, Northfield, MN.

"Spirited Celebrations," p. 44, courtesy of R.G. Moyles.

"Christmas Marketing on the Yukon," p. 45, courtesy of Sunset Publishing Co., Menlo Park, CA.

"Gold Bottom Christmas," p. 55, courtesy of the *Alaskan Philatelist,* The Official Publication of the Alaska Collectors Club, vol. xi, no. 6, whole number 64.

"St. Paul's Church Archival Records," p. 66, courtesy of Synod of the Diocese of Yukon. Yukon Archives, Anglican Church Collection.

"First Christmas in Atlin City," p. 69, courtesy of T.D. Sanders.

"Bennett News," p. 76, courtesy of *Whitehorse Star,* Whitehorse, Y.T.

"A Klondike Wedding, Christmas Day 1904," p. 77, courtesy of John Bell Pringle and Mary Pringle Jamieson.

"Klondike Party," p. 87, courtesy of R.C. Coutts.

"Christmas in Old Crow," p. 101, courtesy of Myra and Mark Ryder.

"Sixty and Seventy Below," p. 105, courtesy of Shoe String Press, North Haven, CT.

"Turkey Shoot at Carcross," p. 110, courtesy of *Whitehorse Star,* Whitehorse, Y.T.

"Sourdough Story," p. 115, courtesy of John Bell Pringle and Mary Pringle Jamieson.

"Christmas Along the Trail," p. 121, courtesy of *Whitehorse Star,* Whitehorse, Y.T.

Photo Credits

p. 1: from *Alaska and the Klondike* by Angelo Heilprin. London: C. Arthur Pearson, 1899.

p. 6: courtesy of Nancy Moulton.

p. 10: from *In to the Yukon* by William Seymour Edwards. Cincinnati: The Robert Clark Co., 1904.

p. 38: courtesy of Ezekiel Enterprises, Whitehorse, Yukon. Yukon Archives, Anglican Church Collection.

p. 50: courtesy of Nancy Moulton.

p. 55: from *Two Years in the Klondike and Alaskan Goldfields* by William Haskell. Hartford, Conn.: Hartford Publishing, 1898.

p. 58: from *Two Years in the Klondike and Alaskan Goldfields* by William Haskell. Hartford, Conn.: Hartford Publishing, 1898.

p. 68: courtesy of Ezekiel Enterprises, Whitehorse, Yukon. Yukon Archives, Hamilton Collection.

p. 82: from *In to the Yukon* by William Seymour Edwards. Cincinnati: The Robert Clark Co., 1904.

p. 106: from *Alaska and the Klondike* by J.S. McLain. New York: McClure, Phillips & Co., 1905.

p. 112: from *In to the Yukon* by William Seymour Edwards. Cincinnati: The Robert Clark Co., 1904.

p. 115: from *Through the Gold Fields of Alaska to the Bering Straits* by H. DeWindt. Harper & Brother, 1898.

Text Sources

Armstrong, Nevill. *Yukon Yesterdays.* London: John Long, 1936. pp. 254–55.

Berton, Laura Beatrice. *I Married the Klondike.* Toronto: McClelland & Stewart, 1967. pp. 60–63.

Bobillier, Father Marcel. "Madame Emilie Tremblay: A pioneer woman of the Yukon." Unpublished manuscript, date unknown. pp. 26–28.

Bompas, Charlotte. "Christmas 100 years ago," *Five Pioneer Women of the Anglican Church in the Yukon.* Whitehorse: Yukon Diocesan Board, Women's Auxiliary of the Anglican Church of Canada, 1964.

Camsell, Charles. "Klondike Madness." *Son of the North.* Toronto: Ryerson Press, 1954. pp. 67–68.

Carey, Mary (Edith Tyrrell). "The First Klondike Baby." *Gold Magazine.* 1933. pp. 8–9.

Carmack, George. *Klondike News.* Dawson, Y.T. April 1898.

"Christmas Along the Trail." Christmas booklet, *Whitehorse Star.* 1966.

"Christmas at Bennett, 1901." Christmas booklet, *Whitehorse Star.* 1966.

"Christmas at Carcross in 1901." Christmas booklet, *Whitehorse Star.* 1966.

"Christmas in the Klondike." Author unknown. Unpublished manuscript, Coutts Collection, Yukon Archives. Whitehorse, Y.T.

Craig, Lulu Alice. *Glimpses of Sunshine and Shade in the Far North.* Cincinnati, OH: Editor Publishing Co., 1900. pp. 72–73.

Crawford, Jack. Unpublished Christmas card, 1898. Special Collections, University of Washington Libraries, Neg. #UW 2791.

"Dance Goes Merrily On." *The Yukon Sun.* Dawson, Y.T. December 27, 1903.

DeGraf, Anna. "Sixty and Seventy Below." *Pioneering on the Yukon 1892–1917.* Roger S. Brown, ed. New Haven, CT: The Shoe String Press, 1992. pp. 83–84.

Fenton, Faith. "In Dawson City." *The Globe.* Toronto. Early 1899.

——, ed. *The Paystreak.* Dawson, Y.T. December 25, 1899.

Ferry, Eudora Bundy. "Christmas." *Yukon Gold.* Jericho, NY: Exposition Press, 1971. pp. 56–58.

Haskell, William. "A Homelike Fireside." *Two Years in the Klondike and Alaskan Gold Fields.* Hartford, CT: Hartford Publishing, 1898. pp. 302–4.

———. pp. 301–2.

Hubbard, Samuel Jr. "Christmas Marketing on the Yukon." *Sunset Magazine.* Date unknown. pp. 122–24.

Isaac, Gerald and V.H. *Moosehide: An oral history.* Dawson, Y.T.: Yukon College, Dawson Campus, 1994. pp. 34, 91.

Klondike Nugget, The. Dawson, Y.T. December 1898.

Kutz, Kenneth J. Letter by unknown writer, 1897. *Klondike Gold.* Darien, CT: Gold Fever Publishing, 1996.

Lokke, Carl. *Klondike Saga.* Northfield, MN: Norwegian-American Historical Association, 1965. pp. 134–37.

London, Jack. "A Klondike Christmas." *The Complete Short Stories of Jack London.* Stanford, CA: Stanford University Press, 1993. pp. 150–55.

Lynch, Jeremiah. *Three Years in the Klondike.* Chicago: R.R. Donnelly & Sons, 1967. pp. 69–70.

McAdam, Ebenezer. *From Duck Lake to Dawson City: The Diary of Ebenezer McAdam's Journey to the Klondike, 1898–1899.* R.G. Moyles, ed.. Saskatoon, Sask.: Western Producer Prairie Books, 1977. pp. 68–71.

McQuesten, Leroy. "Christmas at Fort Reliance, 1882." Christmas booklet, *Whitehorse Star.* 1966.

Money, Anton with Ben East. *This Was the North.* Toronto: General Publishing Co., 1975. pp. 123–30.

Pringle, George. *Adventures in Service.* Toronto: McClelland & Stewart, 1929. pp. 104–7.

———. "Sourdough Story." *Western Recorder Magazine.* Vancouver, B.C. December 1943.

Ryder-Tidd, Claude and Mary. "Christmas in Old Crow." *Life in the Yukon.* Lancaster, PA: Myra and Mark Ryder, Publishers, 1993. pp. 58–59.

Service, Robert. "The Cremation of Sam McGee." *Collected Poems of Robert Service.* New York: Dodd, Mead & Co., 1961. pp. 33–36.

———. "The Trapper's Christmas Eve." *Collected Poems of Robert Service.* New York: Dodd, Mead & Co., 1961. pp. 242–43.

Shore, Evelyn Berglund. "A Northern Childhood." *Born on Snowshoes.* Cambridge, MA: Houghton Mifflin Co., 1954. pp. 18–20.

Stables, Gordon. "Christmas in Klondyke." *Off to Klondyke or A Cowboy's Rush to the Gold Fields.* London: James Nisbet & Co., 1898. pp. 280–81.

Sutherland, Howard V. "December." *Out of the North.* New York: Desmond Fitzgerald Inc., 1913. p. 7.

Trelawney-Anselm, E.C. *I Followed Gold,* London: Peter Davis, 1938. p. 179.

Warren, James R.H. "Christmas Greetings from St. Paul's Church, Dawson Y.T." Christmas card, 1902. Whitehorse, Y.T.

Wells, E. Hazard. "The Escape." *Magnificence and Misery: A firsthand account of the 1897 Klondike Gold Rush.* Randall M. Dodd, ed. Garden City, NY: Doubleday & Co., 1984. pp. 170–71.

White, William. "First Christmas in Atlin City." *Writing Home.* Exeter, Essex: T.D. Sanders, Publisher, 1990. pp. 68–72.

About the Editor

Anne Tempelman-Kluit is an award-winning author who has written extensively about Yukon people and places. She was a political reporter and feature writer for the *Whitehorse Star* and the Yukon columnist for *The Globe and Mail*. Anne has written for many national and local publications, including *Chatelaine, Equinox, Harrowsmith, The Financial Post Magazine, Beautiful British Columbia Magazine, Vancouver Magazine,* and *The Vancouver Sun*. She is also the author of *Discover Canada: Yukon* and *Green Spaces of Vancouver*.

Dirk Tempelman-Kluit

Born and educated in Britain, Anne has lived in Canada since 1961. She first visited the Yukon in 1964 and subsequently lived and travelled throughout the territory. She spent three months rafting down the Yukon River, walked the North Canol Road and covered the thousand-mile Iditarod sled dog race across Alaska. Anne now lives in Vancouver and visits the Yukon as often as she can.